Negril Beach Vacations

A comprehensive guide for travelers to Seven Mile Beach Negril, Jamaica

by Scott Hansen

All rights reserved. No part of this book may be reproduced in any form or by any electronic or mechanical means, including information storage and retrieval systems, without written permission from the author, except in the case of a reviewer, who may quote brief passages embodied in critical articles or in a review.

Trademarked names appear throughout this book. Rather than use a trademark symbol with every occurrence of a trademarked name, names are used in an editorial fashion, with no intention of infringement of the respective owner's trademark.

The information in this book is distributed on an "as is" basis, without warranty. Although every precaution has been taken in the preparation of this work, neither the author nor the publisher shall have any liability to any person or entity with respect to any loss or damage caused or alleged to be caused directly or indirectly by the information contained in this book.

Scott Hansen

3nd Edition

© 2014 by Scott Hansen

scotthanse@gmail.com

Table of Contents

Acknowledgements 6
Preface 7
Getting There and What to Expect 11
Transportation to and from the Airport 15
Money 22
Food, Alcohol and Water 25
    Alcohol and cigarettes 27
    Water 28
Other Important Information 29
    Electronics 29
    What to pack 29
    Ganja, marijuana, Mary Jane, etc. 31
    Taxis and other ground transportation 33
    The Weather 34
    Calling Jamaica 35
Seven Mile Beach 36
Places to Eat 46
    Restaurants on Seven Mile Beach 47
    Restaurants on the Cliffs or West End 51
    Restaurants in the Town of Negril 55
Things to Do in and Around Negril 58
Where to Stay 66
Map of Hotels on Seven Mile Beach, Negril Jamaica 69
    North 69

Map Key 69
Hotels, Hostels, Villas, Cottages, and Cabins on Seven Mile Beach, Negril 76
Hotels Listed Alphabetically. 79
Hotels with Links to Web Pages and Contact Information Listed Alphabetically. 84
    Amenities Key: 84
    Hotels with Amenities List 84
Negril Jamaica Checklist 130
Contact the Author 133

Acknowledgements

In the process of writing a travel book, and then putting out new editions, an author often gets great feedback and help from his or her readers. I have been lucky enough to have had a few people write to me with great ideas on how to make this book better. I agree with most of their observations. People who go to Negril love Jamaica and its people. We love the beach, sand, water, and the general atmosphere that this island paradise provides for travelers. We tend to let everyone we know and come in contact with how much we enjoyed our vacations and we let them know the good things that Negril and Jamaica have to offer.

I would like to thank Bill Lurvery for his email giving me advice on how to improve some sections of my book and to include things I have omitted. Thank you.

I would also like to thank one hotel owner whose name I lost, I am so sorry, who gave me a complete and updated list of the hotels on Seven Mile Beach. A lot of the hotels are run by families and frequently change names. This person sent me the most current list that he knew about and it was very helpful.

I would like to thank the other hotel owners and managers whom I have emailed requesting information about their hotel and anything else they want to add about Negril.

Finally, I would like to thank the people of Negril. Thank you for sharing the beauty of your beaches and the beauty of your island.

Preface

Negril is a very cool and funky little village on the West end of the island of Jamaica. The places to stay there are usually family run and small but they do have a few big all-inclusive resorts as well. Places change names all the time and are sold to other people all the time and things change. This book is the third edition of my book and it is as up-to-date as possible as of the publishing. Every effort has been made to confirm and verify the existence and name of the resorts and hotels in Negril as well as up-to-date contact information. It is hard to get definitive information online and that is the reason I wrote this book, to have everything you need to know about Negril's Seven Mile Beach in one easy to read book.

I took my first trip to Negril, Jamaica in the summer of 2006 and I immediately fell in love with the place. I went there with a friend I used to work with and we stayed at a place he knew called Lazy Dayz. The place was right on Seven Mile Beach and it was rustic and simple and one of the most beautiful places I ever stayed at. I knew I was in love.

Our days consisted of petting the dog that lived there, Mayfee, who has shuffled off this mortal coil, drinking fresh squeezed juice in the morning bought from a beach vendor, reading on the white sand beach, and finding dinner at any place within walking distance along Seven Mile Beach. I decompressed quickly on that trip. Mayfee would spend her time chasing away Rastas and greeting everyone else with a wag of the tail and generally looking for affection.

I have been back almost every year since then. I have stayed on Bloody Bay, which is directly north of Seven Mile Beach and consists mostly of all-inclusive resorts, and I have stayed in some places that are a little more rustic. Bloody Bay is only separated by Seven Mile Beach by a rocky outcropping, making it a little hideaway in and of itself.

Whether you decide to stay in a rustic little cottage or at an all-inclusive resort, you will have a wonderful time in Negril. Both options have their charms, although to me an all-inclusive is the same there as it is in Mexico or the Dominican Republic. For the true Negril I usually stay at the smaller resorts but I will discuss both options in this book. I would not mind if the rest of my vacations were in Negril.

This book is dedicated to Seven Mile Beach in Negril Jamaica, only. If you are interested in other places in Jamaica then this book is not for you. I do not know enough about the Cliffs of Negril (the West End) to include the hotels in this edition, although I have tried several restaurants there. There are many fine hotels and villas in the Cliffs that have the charm of old Negril. I prefer to walk directly on the beach.

I have written this book for an audience that has never been to Jamaica, who have never been to Negril, and for people who are considering traveling to Jamaica but were scared off by stories about the place. Even if you have been to Negril you will find helpful information about the place. I have never felt unsafe in Negril and my experiences with the people there have always been positive. Negril is a town and beach that is set up for tourists and they do not want their reputation tarnished. If you take normal travel precautions you should be safe in your travels there as well.

When I was planning my various trips I noticed there was not a lot of great information about Negril all in one place. I had a lot of questions and I had to do a lot of research in order to figure out what I needed to know about going there. I put together this book out of love and I hope it shows through. I also put this book together to help other people take the plunge and visit one of the most beautiful places on earth.

I have written this book like you would hear about a trip from a friend. It is written deliberately in a conversational style and is an easy read. Do not let this fool you; there is also a lot of practical and useful information in this book. If you enjoy it only 10% as much as I enjoyed researching and writing it, then that would make me one happy author.

Eire!

Scott Hansen

Figure 1 Me on Seven Mile Beach enjoying a Red Stripe

Getting There and What to Expect

The closest airport to Negril, Jamaica is in Montego Bay (the airport code is MBJ). The airport is about an hour and a half north of Negril if you are travelling by car, and you will have to hire a taxi or ride in a bus to get from the airport to Negril. The fare is about $60-70 per trip, $120 to $140 round trip, in U.S. Dollars as of this writing (all currency mentioned in this book are in U.S. dollars). The more people you travel with, the cheaper your transportation becomes. I have included a list of transportation options in the next chapter, "Transportation to and from the Airport," which is a big list, but by no means complete. All of the transportation options listed in the next chapter are recommended on various travel sites and are used by other travelers; be sure to check the web sites or contact information before you go, because even these things change in Negril. If you travel to Negril more than once you will find yourself using the same person for your airport transfers because they become like a family to you. I personally use a man named Rocky, who in addition to the cab ride, offers the use of a cell phone for the week. Using a local cell phone and buying an international phone card at the Hi-Lo is cheaper than using your own cell phone to make calls back home.

Jamaica is located next to Cuba in the Caribbean so your flight times will depend on where you depart. You will most likely fly over Cuba which is kind of a neat experience. The water in the Caribbean is as pretty and blue as any postcard you have seen.

When your plane lands you will need to go through customs and you will be presented with options to change your money. Do not change your money at the airport. You will get a much better rate at the Hi-Lo in town or any of the Cambios, or if you want to risk it, from individuals on the street who offer much better rates of exchange. I do not change any money at all; I simply bring US currency in small denominations to get me through my week.

When you get through customs you will need to get your luggage. I would suggest you have a pair of shorts and a t-shirt in your carry-on bag, and while waiting for your luggage arrive, go and change clothes in the rest room. It is very warm and humid in Jamaica and you will notice the heat immediately and there is no reason to be uncomfortable on your hour and a half drive.

When you come out of the terminal you will be assaulted by taxi drivers who are willing to take you anywhere. If you did not book a taxi or ride ahead of time then feel free to negotiate with the drivers for a ride to your hotel in Negril, or go to the bus counter in the terminal to book a ride on a bus for about $20. If you have made arrangements you will find your driver standing outside holding a sign with your name on it.

Always make sure the taxi has current license plates and are insured. All registered taxis in Jamaica have a red license plate with white numbers so be sure to hire a driver that is registered.

You will also be surrounded by people who want to take your bags for you and who will offer to help you load the bags in your cab. I usually let people do this for me and I tip them $1.00 per bag, U.S. Jamaica is a poor country and the money they earn here will help them and their families. If you do not want to pay these people or want their help, simply tell them firmly, "No thank you."

Also, when you step out into the heat of Jamaica, you will be offered a Red Stripe beer or another drink of your choice. You will pay a premium at the airport, about $5.00 a bottle because the person bringing you the drink is basically hiring himself out as a waiter. If you wait, your driver will sometimes have a nice cold beer for you when you get off the plane and into his taxi. You can also tough it out and wait until you get to your hotel before having your first drink.

Like I mentioned earlier, the taxi ride to Negril is about an hour-and-a-half long ride. If you are prone to motion sickness you should take something for that beforehand because the road is winding and traffic moves slowly through the towns and at a brisk pace when you are in the country. Jamaicans also drive on the left side of the road like they do in Great Britain. If you arrange a taxi ride ahead of time, the same driver who picks you up at the airport will also come to your hotel at the end of your stay to take you back to the airport. Simply tell the driver your departure time and he will tell you when you need to be outside of your hotel ready to travel and head home. This will be the saddest part of your trip.

The road to Negril is fairly new and it hugs the coastline. You will get magnificent views of the ocean as you go along but you will also see a lot of poverty. Be prepared for this. You will soon get used to seeing dogs running around without leashes, goats eating lazily on the side of the road, and skinny cattle tethered to a pole in the middle of a barren field. When you go through the cities like Montego Bay or Ocho Rios, you will see people at every traffic light trying to sell you something. I never buy from these street vendors but I know the locals and the drivers sometimes do.

Jamaica also has a very unique smell to it. It is hard to put into words but it is a mixture of the exotic and island spices. It is tropical. Every time I travel there the smells are so wonderful that it floods my mind with memories of the trips I took there before. Be prepared for your senses to be overloaded.

For such a poor country you will see a lot of new cars driving around, although none of them are American made. For the cab ride to Negril, the driver will play a lot of reggae music the entire trip. On your ride back to the airport you will hear the music that they actually listen to every day and it sounds like a lot of the current music on American radio. For the taxi ride to Negril sit back and relax because you are in Jamaica!

I personally would not travel with children to Negril. If I did, I would certainly stay at an all-inclusive where they will not see as much ganja smoking and adult fun. There is nudity on the beaches (most places allow topless sunbathing and at Hedonism you can go completely nude and there will be many people enjoying an adult beverage or a smoke). Smaller children are usually picky eaters as well and Jamaican cuisine might not be liked by younger children.

Finally the Jamaicans have a language they use called Patois. Patios is a street dialect that you will not understand. The Jamaicans use it when talking to each other. Do not be offended; they are most likely not talking about you, rather they are talking about everyday life. There is a word they use in Patois called "erie." It is pronounced "I-ree." Roughly translated, erie means, "Everything is alright!" Besides being a place on a map, Jamaica is a state of mind. You will always hear the people say, "erie" or "No Problem." Relax, enjoy and get away from it all because you are at one of the most beautiful places on earth.

Erie, mon.

Transportation to and from the Airport

Figure 2 A view from The Negril Beach Club

The following is a list of taxi services and bus services available to get from the airport at Montego Bay to Seven Mile Beach in Negril. JUTA is an organization of private bus, taxi or limo services that provide transportation to and from the airport. You do not need reservations to book one at the airport, but I always like to plan ahead. JUTA has a counter at the airport if you need transportation. There are many other options to choose from, but the ones listed below all have been given great reviews from travelers to Negril. Always check the websites before you go and if you decide to hire someone, you will set this up via emails before your trip.

Big Ship Tours:

www.bigshiptours.com

Phone: 876-722-8759

Email: info@bigshiptours.com

Clive's:

www.clivestransportservicejamaica.com.

Phone: 876-956-2615

Cell: 876-869-7571

Email: info@clivestrtansportationservicejamaica.com.

Danny's Island Excursions:

www.dannysislandexcursion.com

Phone: 876-361-3533

Email: dannysisland@gmail.com

Gary's Jamaican Taxi:

http://www.bestjamaicataxi.com/

Phone: 876-776-0800

Cell: 876-826-0292

Gerry's Taxi and Tours:

http://www.gerrystaxiandtoursjamaica.com/

Phone: 876-293-8232

876-427-5870

Email: reservations@gerrystaxiandtours.com

Island Pride Tours:

http://islandpridetours.com/

Phone: 678-995-8262 (US and Canada)

876-472-3119

Email: transfers@islandpridetours.com

Jamaica Exquisite Transfer and Tours:

http://jamaicaexquisitetours.com/

Phone: 954-353-1913 (US and Canada)

876-326-8364

Email: info@jamaicaexquisitetours.com

Jamaica Island Taxi:

http://www.jamaicaislandtaxi.com/

Phone: 876-864-2664

Jamaican Taxi Tours:

http://jamaicantaxitours.com/

Phone: 876-429-8664

876-596-0796

Email: info@jamaicantaxitours.com

Joe Cool Taxi:

www.joecooltaxiandtoursjamaica.com

Phone: 876-390-1614

Email: joecooltaxiandtoursjamaica@gmail.com

Juju Tours:

www.jujutours.com

Phone: 876-833-2921

876-789-4309

Email: info@jujutours.com

JuJuTours@gmail.com

JUTA:

http://www.jutatoursnegrilltd.com/.

Phone: 876-957-9197

876-957-4620

Email: reservations@jutatoursnegrilltd.com

If you are traveling solo or as a couple this may be your best option to get to Negril and save some money. The cost to get to Negril is $20-$25 per person each way and you do not need to book ahead (although I would). They have a counter at the airport and are professional and used heavily by many travelers.

Kenny's Tours:

www.kennytours.com

Phone: 800-204-1466 (US and Canada)

Cell: 876-995-9410

   876-361-2534

Email: Kenny.tours@cwjamaica.com

Kingsley James:

www.kingsleystakecaretours.com

Phone: 876-885-1383

   876-463-0105

PG Tours Jamaica:

http://www.pgtoursja.com/

Phone: 876-450-3648

   876-851-5729

Email: admin@pgtoursja.com

Reggae Tours:

www.reggae-tours.com

Phone: 732-334-0992 (US and Canada)

   876-772-3327

876-772-3327

Cell: 876-570-2983

Fax: 876-631-1019

Email: reservations@reggaetourz.com

Rocky's:

http://rockystaxiandtourservice.com/

Phone: 305-848-8389 (US and Canada)

876-648-1877

Cell: 876-370-7915

Email: roxroy45@hotmail.com

I use Rocky all the time. When you go to Negril you will make many fast friends and keep going back to these people. Rocky has never let me down and gives me a phone to use when I am in Negril. I have heard the same great things about the other taxi services listed here as well.

Turner's Taxis:

http://turnertaxisandtoursjamaica.com/

Phone: 876-461-7452

876-543-3781

Email: reservation@turnertaxisandtoursjamaica.com

Your Jamaican Tour Guide:

www.yourjamaicantourguide.com

Phone: 876-377-7634

Email: info@yourjamaicantourguide.com

Money

The official currency in Jamaica is the Jamaican dollar and everyone calls it the "J". As of this writing one U.S. dollar was worth 111 Jamaican dollars. This means $100.00 U.S. equals about 11,100.00 Jamaican dollars. The exchange rate is very confusing and if you have a phone with an app that has the conversion rate, I would suggest you use it. If you can do the conversion in your head, then more power to you.

I have only exchanged money at the airport the first time I travelled to Negril and I soon found out it was not needed and it was relatively expensive to do so. You do not get a good exchange rate at the airport, but more importantly there is really no need to get Jamaican dollars since the Taxi drivers take U.S. currency. If you are coming from a country other than the US, I would exchange your money at your local bank (at least enough to cover the transportation from the airport), and then when you get to Negril get money out of a cash machine or go to the money exchange in town located at the Hi-Lo grocery store or any other number of Cambios. As a last resort only exchange some of your money at the airport.

A Cambio is a cross between a guy on the street offering to change your money and a bank. They are regulated by the government like banks and are safe. There are several Cambios in Negril and they offer a better exchange rate than the banks but less than the guy on the street. I would NOT exchange money with guys on the street; these people exist and may approach you but stay away from them to be safe. The money exchange I mentioned before in the Hi-Lo, is a Cambio.

On every other trip to Negril since my first trip I never change money. If you stay at an all-inclusive you will need very little money for your transportation to and from the airport and tips for the staff. You can either not spend a thing outside of the all-inclusive or you can arrange excursions through the hotel and use a charge card to pay for it. I usually bring a couple of hundred dollars when I stay at an all-inclusive, in very small denominations, to use to tip the hotel staff, to tip my drivers, to tip the waiters, and to tip the bartenders and enough to cover my transportation costs if I do not prepay them. If you tip the bartender at an all-inclusive $20.00 on your first day, I promise you will get the best service of your life.

When I stay at a hotel on Seven Mile Beach that is not an all-inclusive I always take enough money to get me through my entire trip. I bring about $100 per day per couple, and I bring a lot of ones, a lot of fives and a lot of ten dollar bills. On my last trip my wife and I took $1,000 between us and when we went grocery shopping we used a credit card for groceries. We had plenty of cash to last through the trip and took some home. Everyone you run across, from vendors on the beach to the clerks at the Hi-Lo grocery store, will take U.S. currency. If you give the person a big bill they will give you your change in Jamaican dollars so do not use big bills if at all possible. I keep the bills small in order to not accumulate to much Jamaican money over the course of my trip and of course you can spend the J anywhere on the island. When you travel this way make sure that your room has a working room safe so you can keep all your money in a safe place. I also use my Jamaican dollars that I get in change to tip the maids when I leave.

One other option would be to bring about $200 in U.S. cash in very small denominations and then go to the cash machine in town to get money for the rest of your trip. You simply need to be careful to not take out too much money and have to exchange it back before you leave because this will cost you money in the exchange fees. You will also most likely pay a high fee for this service, and that is why I avoid it.

I always tip the maids who clean up my room whether I am staying at an all-inclusive or a hotel on the beach. I usually tip them $20 for every week I stay there. They always will keep your room clean and they work hard for their money. They are also poor and they really appreciate the extra money. If I am not staying at an all-inclusive I ask the maid if she would like my empty beer bottles because they can turn them in and get the deposit back. Usually they want them, and it is like giving them a bigger tip.

Finally, I usually give my maid all the extra Jamaican dollars or change that I have left over from the week. Since I try to keep the amount of Jamaican dollars I have to a minimum, this usually is not much more than a couple of dollars US. The money you leave your maids has a very direct and positive impact on their lives, and to me it is not much money at all.

Food, Alcohol and Water

If you are staying at an all-inclusive you will not need to worry about food, drink or water because it will all be provided for you. This section is geared towards those who stay at a hotel or villa on the beach.

Food in Jamaica is expensive. Jamaica is an island and they have to import almost all their food in from somewhere else. When I stay at a hotel on the beach I always make sure there is at least a refrigerator for me to use and I also like to have a little kitchenette if possible. The first thing I do when I arrive is either walk into town or take a taxi and go grocery shopping.at the Hi-Lo. I stock up on things I think I will need for the whole week.

I also bring food with me when I travel to Jamaica if I am not staying at an all-inclusive. Since food is so expensive there, you can defray some of your travel costs by bringing your own food and alcohol. I usually bring a jar of unopened peanut butter and a jar of unopened jelly for peanut butter and jelly sandwiches. You must keep things like these unopened in order to get through customs. I also bring a carton of granola bars, snack foods, cookies, candy bars and whatever else that comes prepackaged and that you may crave on your trip. Make sure all the food you bring does not significantly add to the weight of your luggage because you will pay dearly for this if you go over your allowed baggage weight. The great thing about bringing your own food is that when you use up the food you bring with you, at the same time you will make room in your suitcase for the souvenirs you buy in Jamaica.

Things I buy at the Hi-Lo grocery store in town are things like breakfast cereals, milk, eggs (if you have a stove to cook them on), beer, breakfast sausages, and things you like to eat and are easy to make. I buy bread and pasta sauce if we want to eat pasta one night. I buy an international calling card for the cell phone that my taxi driver lets me use. I buy any snacks I think I will need except for the things I bring in from home and I buy a couple bottled waters which I refill in my hotel room.

Do not buy any fruit at the store. There are vendors selling fruit every day on the beach. The fruit is fresh, they will cut it for you, and you can also get a liter of freshly squeezed juices for about $4.00 U.S. There is nothing better than fresh cut fruit on the beach. The vendors sell fruit that is better than in the super market and they have a bigger variety, and they are usually about the same price as at the grocery store. The fruit looks better than what is in the grocery store and you are providing a living to the women who sell fruit on the beach.

During lunch time on the beach you will see a man pushing a decrepit looking bike with no seat and with a big metal cooler on the front handlebars. He is selling patties. My friend described patties as Jamaican hamburgers. They are stuffed with several different things like hamburger meat which is a little spicy, or chicken, or vegetarian, or any other ingredient the Jamaicans feel like putting in it. The patties are wonderful tasting and they are cheap. You can usually buy three patties, which will easily feed two people, for about $5.00 U.S. Do not be put off by the food delivery system; the patties are baked fresh each morning and they really do taste great.

Also when you get to Negril you will notice a lot of people on the side of the road with big metal drum BBQ smokers. These men and women are cooking jerk chicken and the taste is absolutely fantastic. The people who cook jerk these chickens have been doing it for years and they know what they are doing. You will find that different stands that have different ideas of what jerk chicken should taste like and the spices are different. If you sample enough jerk chicken stands, you will find a cook that really makes your taste buds happy. You can get a half chicken for about $10 U.S. and that will easily feed a couple for lunch or dinner. You can also buy a quarter chicken for $5 U.S. The chicken is served with a slice of white bread and some jerk chicken sauce. It is a very inexpensive way to get dinner or lunch on Seven Mile Beach and the taste is phenomenal.

There are also many different restaurants in Negril from casual to fancy. If you will be going out to eat at a nicer place you will need a pair of nice pants and a nice shirt if you are a man and something dressy if you are a woman. There are a lot of places to eat right on the beach. Just walk up and grab a table and you will be waited on fairly quickly at most places. You could also take a taxi into town or to the cliffs to eat. The food in Jamaica is very good, but do not get a hamburger down there because you will most likely be disappointed. Most food from your home country will not quite taste the same in Jamaica, but that is part of the charm.

Alcohol and cigarettes

Alcohol is usually expensive in Jamaica, except for rum. You can bring up to two liters of alcohol per person into Jamaica, as well as two cartons of cigarettes. If you smoke, cigarettes are very expensive there as well. My wife always brings a large 1.75 liter bottle of Vodka with her from home and this brings her alcohol costs way down. She mixes the vodka with fresh squeezed fruit juice that she buys on the beach. I drink beer so I get cases of Red Strip at the Hi-Lo. Red Stripe costs more to buy in Negril than it does for me to buy it at my local liquor store. You will also have to pay a deposit on each bottle of beer you buy. When you bring in your own bottle liquor you will also have more room in your suitcase when it is time to go home.

My wife has also started packing a mixer on our trips to Jamaica. The mixer she owns has a cooler that is used to do the mixing in. You throw your ice, alcohol and juice in the blender, mix it up, and then take the top cooler to the beach for the afternoon. It is quick and convenient and she would not travel to Jamaica without it.

If you run out of cigarettes there are plenty of people selling cigarettes and cigars on the beach. These are often cheaper than buying them in the stores and like everything else in Negril the price is negotiable.

Water

When travelling to Jamaica you do not need to worry about drinking the water. Jamaica has water treatment plants like they do in the U.S. and you can drink right from the tap. If you prefer bottled water they sell it at the Hi-Lo or any other store in town. I usually buy a couple of small bottles of water at the store and refill them in my room. This will help cut down on your water costs.

Other Important Information

Electronics

The electricity in Jamaica is 110 volt and you can run anything you do in the United States in the outlets in Negril. You do not need to buy a converter if coming from the U.S. If you come from the U.K you will need to buy a converter to get your computer or other electronics to run.

Wi-Fi is becoming more popular every time I visit Jamaica. Ask at the resort you are staying at if they have the internet and Wi-Fi available for the guests or look at the guide I provided in the last chapter of this book. Sometimes you will have to go to common areas, like a lobby or poolside, to access the internet. Keep in mind you are in a public area and you are connecting to the internet over public airwaves so use any precautions you would use at a coffee shop in the United States.

What to pack

The following is a basic guide to what you will need in Jamaica. Various people have various needs so this list is intended to be used as a guideline and not as the final word. You probably will need things that I have not thought to put on the list.

Money is the first thing you should not forget to bring. I would also pack a credit card. Traveler's checks are not common anymore because most people go to the ATM at the bank in town. There are also ATMs long the road that runs next to Seven Mile Beach. I bring a lot of little bills because it is easier for Jamaicans to make change with them and they are great for tips. All the change you will get back will be in Jamaican Dollars, or J's.

Here is the absolute minimum you will need for clothes. Bring a swimsuit because that is the main reason for choosing Negril, is it not? You can get by at most dining places with shorts and a shirt. A nice pair of slacks and one dress shirt should get you into any fancier restaurants. At night it can cool off and get breezy so it is worthwhile to pack a sweater or a light jacket for the times when the sun goes down. My wife usually brings one nice dress and the rest of her clothes are casual and built around her swimsuits. Sandals are worn everywhere and you rarely see black dress shoes except on some of the women. Pack underwear and socks to get you through your trip. If you like to exercise be sure to bring your workout clothes.

Keep in mind that things will not completely dry if you leave them on your patio overnight. This is because Jamaica is a humid place. It is tropical. There is heat, humidity, bugs, and the occasional rain shower. It could be a good idea to bring two swimsuits and alternate them every other day.

Overall Negril is extremely laid back and you can get by wearing shorts and a t-shirt at most places. You will spend most of your time on the beach in your swimsuit so you do not need to worry about packing a lot of clothes.

Next, bring sunscreen. You will need plenty of it because the sun it hot and relentless on the beach and in the water. You will need to reapply several times a day to make sure you do not get a burn. The surest way to ruin a vacation is to get bad sunburn and have to be in pain the entire week. Sunscreen is very expensive to buy in Jamaica. You are better bringing more than you think you will need, than less. If you are prone to burning bring at least an SPF 50 sunscreen. Make sure the sunscreen is water and sweat proof because you most likely will be going in the ocean or pool. Even if you tan I would bring a high SPF sunscreen as to not burn. You will get color on Seven Mile Beach.

Be sure to pack sun glasses as well. The sun is bright and you will be in the water a lot, too. Bring a decent pair of glasses, but a pair that you do not care if they get lost. I always bring an older pair and I always bring ones that have UV protection. Keep in mind if you do lose them you can always buy another pair from a vendor on the beach. The sunglasses they sell on the beach tend to be very cheap if you bargain, and you tend to get what you pay for.

Pack a beach towel if you decide to stay in one of the more rustic accommodations. If you do not feel like packing a towel there are many, many vendors on the beach that will sell you a towel for about $10 US. Remember to bargain with them and do not accept their marked prices even in stores that have four walls and a roof.

Pack your toiletries and any prescription medication you may have. There are a couple of drug stores in Negril if you absolutely need something you did not pack, but things tend to be expensive down there.

Pack a collapsible cooler with a re-freezable ice pack so that your drinks do not get warm on the beach. Like I mentioned before, my wife packed a blender that is made by Hamilton Beach that has a cooler attachment as well as a glass attachment. The cooler attachment is light and it keeps your drinks cold. You will not need to pack the glass attachment. It does not take up much space in the suitcase and it will not weigh you down too much. It was a great call on her part to pack this very useful item. You can find this item on the internet if you want to purchase it.

If you smoke or plan to smoke bring a lighter to Jamaica but be sure to pack it in your suitcase as to not get it taken away at the airport. If you forget, lighters are not very expensive in Negril but they do cost more than you would pay for a lighter in the States.

I have also included a checklist of what to pack at the end of this book.

Ganja, marijuana, Mary Jane, etc.

I am not in any way, shape or form encouraging you to smoke or do drugs in this book; that is a personal choice that you will have to make. I am only providing information to you and you can do what you want with the information provided.

Right now, June 2014, marijuana is illegal in Jamaica. If you get caught they can throw you in jail and that would really cramp your vacation style.

As of this writing, however, I read that the government is working to decriminalize marijuana for anyone having less than two ounces, which is more than enough for a few people for a week of fun. In the future, if you get caught with anything under two ounces they are proposing a fine and no criminal charges. I expect this will happen sometime in late 2014. This is long overdue in a country that is known for growing marijuana. Check the internet to see if this measure passed and has become law and if that is the case the threat of going to jail for smoking ganja will be gone.

That being said, ganja is readily available in Jamaica even as of this writing. You will be approached on the beach every day you are there, and you will be approached multiple times. There is always a story and it usually involves a cousin or brother who has crops in the mountains and who has the best stuff on the islands. If you turn the people down they will offer you mushrooms, cocaine, hash and various other drug products I have never heard of before. The quest to sell you ganja and other illegal drugs will be relentless because this is a poor country. People will come up to you on the beach and say, "Respect," which loosely translates to, "Buy something from me." If you are firm, and you say no and keep walking, then you will be left alone.

You can get a large baggie of marijuana for about $20 U.S. As with every other item in Negril be sure to haggle, it is expected. People around you will be smoking joints on the beach, but it is always done discretely. If you decide to purchase $20 worth of ganja it will easily supply six people for a weeks' worth of fun and you will have plenty left over to give to someone else when you leave Jamaica.

Buying Ganga at the all-inclusives is a bit more daunting because the all-inclusive resorts do not like peddlers on their beaches. The security guards frown on people selling drugs on their property and smoking there. The easiest way around this is to simply walk the beach. You soon will be offered many different kinds and types of marijuana in which you can enjoy. If you smoke it discretely you will be left alone.

You can buy smoking paper or pipes to smoke the ganja, in the little souvenir shops that dot the beach. It would be a good idea to buy something cheap and that you can throw away when you leave the country. If you have a pipe that you used with even trace amounts of marijuana left in the bowl, the dogs at the airport when you return will find it for sure and this could lead to a lot of hassle for you. It is illegal to sell screens for the pipes in Jamaica, so if you smoke go to a head shop in the U.S. and buy some screens for a pipe.

You can buy papers for rolling your own joints at any number of places along the beach.

Taxis and other ground transportation

Just another note on using Taxis in Negril: If you walk along the main road in Negril you will get honked at and asked if you need a ride. Government regulated taxis <u>ALWAYS</u> have a red license plate with white numbers and one of the numbers is always a 9. These taxis have to pay a fee to the government for being a taxi service and have to be insured and they are always the safest way to travel in Jamaica.

Other cars pose as taxis and sometimes it can be dangerous to get in one of them. I was told of a couple who got in an unlicensed taxi and they were taken away and robbed in a remote part of the island. Always travel safe in Negril and use common sense and if something makes you feel uncomfortable then trust your instincts.

Some restaurants on the Cliffs and the West End will cover the cost of a taxi to get to their place of business, since the vast majority of people stay on Seven Mile Beach. You usually will have to pay for your own ride back, although some places provide round trip service. When making reservations ask the restaurant if they offer this service, it is worth a shot. Tip the drivers nonetheless because that is what is expected.

Before you get in a taxi always get the price up front. There are no meters and sometimes you can negotiate (they might bring down the price if they can drive you round trip). The following are guidelines for what it cost to ride in a Taxi in Negril. The price is the same whether it is one person in the car or four.

The cost of a taxi from anywhere on Seven Mile Beach to anywhere else on Seven Mile Beach, or into town (which abuts Seven Mile Beach), is $5.00 U.S. not including tip. This is for up to four people.

It costs $5.00 to go anywhere from the cliffs to the cliffs.

The cost to travel between Seven Mile Beach and the Cliffs is $10 U.S. each way, not including tip.

Transportation to and from the airport is between $60-$70 U.S. each way. The more people you travel with, the lower your cost per person. JUTA is the exception and if you are traveling solo or as a couple it would be cheaper to use this taxi service.

The Weather

The weather in Jamaica is usually warm and tropical making it the perfect getaway for those long winter months. The summer months are hotter but only by a few degrees.

Cooler weather in Jamaica is from December to April, but cooler is a relative term. I live in Minnesota so these winter temperatures are hot and feel nice. Expect highs in the upper 80's during these months.

The rainy season is from the end of April to early October. It can rain any part of the day but most days it simply rains in the later afternoon and early into the evening.

The Hurricane season is from June to October. Negril has experienced hurricanes in the past even though it is on the Western side of the island and these can be destructive. They are a rare occurrence though, and most likely you will not travel when a hurricane hits.

The dry season is from October through April, although it still can rain. It is usually less humidity this time of year as well.

No matter what time of year you go the weather will be warm, the water and beer will be cool.

Calling Jamaica

When researching this book I sometimes had to get a hold of hotels to confirm if they are still exist or if they are still in business but using only email to communicate. I have had to call Jamaica a few times and it is not cheap if you use your cell phone or your home phone. I have found the cheapest route is to get a calling card from Walmart or Target. I purchased a $10 international calling card from AT&T and it gave me 64 minutes of calling time to Negril. These minutes never expire. That works out to about $0.16 a minute.

I researched my home cost to call Jamaica and it was $1.78 a minute during business hours. My cell phone company charges me $1.49 a minute to call Jamaica. That is too much money.

You do not need to dial a special country code when calling Jamaica. Simply dial a 1 and then the phone number with the 876 prefix. The connections I have had have been very high quality.

When you get to Negril my taxi driver, Rocky, lets me use a cell phone for the week. Ask your transportation driver when you contact them if they have a phone you can use when you are in Negril. Phone card minutes can be purchased in town and that brings down your cost to call home.

Seven Mile Beach

Figure 3 Seven Mile Beach Negril, Jamaica

Seven Mile Beach is not exactly seven miles, but it seems like it is. Seven Mile Beach lies just north of the town of Negril and is on the west coast of Jamaica. This makes for some beautiful sunsets. At the northern tip of Seven Mile Beach the beach ends at a rocky outcropping, and just north of that is Bloody Bay. Bloody Bay also has a wonderful white sand beach and it contains a lot of the big all-inclusive resorts in Negril. You can picture the layout of Negril like this: hold up your right hand like you are taking an oath with your palm facing away from you. Spread your thumb out from the rest of the fingers on your hand. The tips of your fingers would be due north on a map. The thumb would be the rocky jetty that separates Seven Mile beach from Bloody Bay. Bloody Bay would be in the space between your thumb and the rest of your hand, and Seven Mile Beach would be represented by the inside line of your arm down to your elbow. The ocean would be to the left of your arm and the rest of Jamaica would be to the right of your arm. Your elbow would mark the approximate location of the town of Negril.

Along Seven Mile beach there are a little less than 100 different resorts, cabins, villas, and hotels to choose from for your stay. Building codes were put in place long ago so that no buildings are allowed that are over three stories tall. The result is that Seven Mile Beach manages to retain a rustic look and feel. Among all your options for places to stay are a wide variety of hotels, hostels, villas, and cabins. I have includes a list of all the places you can stay at in later chapters. If I missed any, please contact me via email and I will include it in my next edition. I have also included a rough idea of how these places were rated by travelers that I culled from several different sources, including my own travels.

Also included in this book is a visual guide that lets you know what amenities are at each resort, along with the number of rooms. This will help you get a better idea of what you are getting into when you go to Negril. Many places, probably the majority of places, would be described as rustic in the U.S. They are four walls and a roof with few creature comforts but are perfect if you are in search of a place to crash and you plan on being on the beach all day.

A lot of times you will call or read about a hotel and you will be told it is up to American standards. This means that the electrical wires are buried behind sheetrock, the place is usually kept well-painted and everything in the room works as expected. These places would be the three or four star resorts in Jamaica and you will pay more money to stay in them. These places are much like a room at a Days Inn in the United States; the rooms are basic and functional.

Other places, like the cabins, are more rustic. I have stayed in a place that has rooms that are built like a tree house. Every room is built up in the trees and the rooms have no air conditioning. The rooms did have a refrigerator, a ceiling fan and a bed, but the bathroom was in a separate structure next to the room, up in the trees. The showers looked like they were out of Gilligan's Island. It was one of the most beautiful places I have stayed and I would go there again in a heartbeat. It is called Lazy Dayz and I mentioned it earlier in this book.

I have also stayed at places that my uptight neighbors in suburbia poo-pooed because it was not up to their standards. You could see that the place needed a paint job. The wires were tacked onto the walls. The bathrooms were older and showing wear. The kitchenettes were well-worn but functional. This place might get a one star in the U.S. but it is one of my favorite places to stay. This place gets three stars in Jamaica. I did not mind the looks of that room at all. Why? I am only in my room at night to sleep. As long as I have a clean bed, clean sheets, and running hot water I am happy. The place was safe and inexpensive.

The place is called Negril Beach Club and it has the best beach on all of Negril's Seven Mile Beach because the beach is expansive and deep and filled with palm and other trees for shade. The beach is about 100 yards deep at this resort where it is usually only 30 or 40 feet deep at the most in other places. The water in front of The Negril Beach Club has just a little coral and a lot of sand. The hotel itself is only a ten minute walk to town, meaning it is on the south end of Seven Mile Beach. This place is both a hotel and condos that people own and rent out.

Villas or condos are usually the most expensive accommodations when staying in Negril. There are a few that are right on Seven Mile Beach and if you get a group of people to go down with you then you will bring the cost way down. Most of these Villas and Condos are very nice and up to American standards for quality and cleanliness. Most of them have several different buildings and each building has a different number of bedrooms in them. The villas always have nice appliances and a kitchen to use. A group of people can live communally for the week if this is what you desire. Some large villas have several bedrooms they rent out and communal kitchens and living rooms.

All-inclusive resorts are usually the most expensive accommodations but this is because all of your food and liquor costs are paid for in advance. It is a great way to travel if you do not want to carry a lot of money with you on your trip, or if you want every creature comfort known to man. There is something comforting about buying your ticket and hotel and not have to pay out another penny in costs, except for tips and your transportation to and from the airport. Every room is basically the same and all are air conditioned and up to American standards.

Hotel costs are factored in a few different ways. If you travel in the middle of winter, November through March, you will pay the high season rates. This is when the tourists come to escape to when temperatures at home are in the single digits. The rates go down significantly in the summer but you also have to contend with hurricane season. I have never been to Negril during the off season but I know the hotel rates are significantly cheaper. I would imagine the flights are cheaper as well but I have never checked into it.

I usually like to rent a place that has a kitchenette for me to use and if they do not have that, at the minimum I need a refrigerator. This will cost you a little more in the price of the room but at the same time it will bring down your food costs because you will eat most of your meals in your room. You will not have to dine out for breakfast, lunch and dinner. It is nice to know if you feel a bit peckish that you can go to your room for a snack.

The beach itself is not very wide in most places, maybe 30 yards from beach to the hotel properties. When high tide is in some parts of the beach are non-existent. There is usually not a lot of shade except under umbrellas that different places put out. Most hotels and resorts hire people to clean the beach first thing every morning so when you get up you will notice everything is raked and the beaches are clean.

The next thing to understand is that a lot of people make their living on the beach. These people sell things. They will usually approach you and say, "Respect," with a fist extended for a fist bump. They will engage you in talk and try to sell you their wares. If you have no intention of buying from them just tell them no. Do not promise you will stop on the way back to your hotel because they will remember you and they will come back to you when they see you on the beach later in the day or even later in the week. You can negotiate on the price of almost anything on the beach and you would be foolish not to do so. It always amazes me how they remember me because they deal with so many different people every day.

It can get annoying to some people to be constantly peppered with requests to buy things. I tend to ignore the sellers so for me it is not an issue. I know people I have traveled with did not like that part of Jamaica. Sometimes the vendors will even wake you up while you are napping on the beach.

There are also a lot of permanent stalls on the beach selling almost anything you need in the way of tourist gifts or knick-knacks. They sell everything from beach towels, wood carvings, t-shirts, and jewelry. When you deal with these sellers you have to negotiate because it is expected. If you do not like to negotiate that is fine too, but the sellers expect it and price their items accordingly. They are on the beach from morning to night selling trinkets to the tourists.

I have also gotten massages on the beach. Most hotels have people they let work the grounds selling massage services. You will pay more in the resort and it will be like getting a massage in the States. If you get a massage on the beach it will most likely be on a mattress or some other homemade massage table. It will be cheaper than in the hotel but in my experiences the massages are just as good as those in a spa setting and the prices are about half what you would pay at a big resort.

A few times a week there is usually a reggae concert at one of the hotels on the beach. People will go up and down the beach with megaphones announcing the shows, the places and the times. A lot of times the hotels will hire Rastas to come and be at the party to help make it more authentic. The concerts are usually crowded but very fun. You will meet a lot of different people and you will most likely smell ganja, and more often than not get offers to partake in the ganja.

Rastafarians, or Rastas are the guys you see wearing dreadlocks and walking the beach. A lot of them sell ganja to make their living. They are usually dressed in bright colors and they are what you expect to see when you go to Jamaica. I had the very unique pleasure of getting to know one Rasta very well. We met a group of ladies who adopted him and every year when they come to Negril they pick him up from his farm in the hills and get him a room at a resort on the beach.

As part of the adoption process they would bring him things like battery operated boom boxes, CDs and other music and they would bring movies on DVD for him to watch in the room. He told me he does not have air conditioning in his home, let alone electricity, and when he stays at the hotel it is truly a vacation for him. He loves tequila and he liked to stay up all night watching Western movies and drinking his tequila, always yelling at the TV screen to movies he has seen before. The ladies said he would be laughing and talking back to the movies all night long. He also said where he lived he had no electricity and when he went to the hotel each year people would steal his things where he lived and the ladies would replenish his supplies. He was one of the nicest human beings I have ever met.

Rastas are vegetarian and a lot of them do not drink, although some do. Every Rasta I have met smoked ganja, though. If you want to take their picture just ask. Some will try to get money out of you but sometimes if you give them a beer they will be happy too. Some will do it for free out of the kindness in their hearts. Rastas are kind of looked down upon by the "normal" people who you will see and interact with every day in Jamaica. I am not sure of the reasoning, but I am sure it has to do with the lifestyle. Like I said earlier, I knew a dog in Negril who did not like Rastas. He liked everyone else in the world, just not Rastas.

From a little after sunrise to sunset, I spend my days on the beach. Your resort will usually have chairs and you may have to get up early and place a towel on the chair you want. At many hotels you will have to play that game even though there are plenty of chairs to go around. The surf is usually calm and relaxing but I have seen it choppy days as well. You will smell everything from suntan oils and lotions to salt coming off the ocean. You will smell foods cooking and the smell of ganja will be everywhere. It is one of the most unique experiences on earth.

We bought coffee off the beach once but it was not good. The quality just was not there. If you want truly good coffee get Blue Moon Coffee from the grocery store. It is expensive, but it is the real deal. The sad part is I can get the same coffee, grown in Jamaica, at my local Costco for about half the price they charge on the island. I have no earthly clue why this is the case.

Do not be afraid to buy food from the vendors or to buy jerk chicken off the street. Unlike Mexico the water in Jamaica is safe to drink and everything you eat, while not up to American restaurant cleanliness standards, is safe and clean. I have never gotten sick in Jamaica and either have my friends who have travelled with me. I have not heard of any traveler who got sick on the food or the water.

During the day you can fulfill almost every single need from vendors on the beach. You do not have to leave your chair except to go to the bathroom. You can buy any souvenirs you may need, you can buy food, drinks, and you can schedule excursions like snorkeling trips or diving trips. People will try to sell you anything. A few of my friends do not like this aspect of Negril very much, but I do. It gives the beach vibrancy. If you do not want what the person is selling tell them no. Be firm. Do not say anything like, "maybe later," or "I left my money in my hotel room." That will give the sellers an opening and they will not forget you or leave you alone and they will be back. No, on the other hand, means no and you will be left alone by that vendor for that day.

The ocean in Negril is warm and wonderful. If you snorkel there is not much coral near the beach, but you can still see some colorful fish and ocean life swimming near you. The water is many different shades of blue and it looks like it was created in Photoshop. The places to eat are painted in bright and vibrant colors and the sails on the boats snap in the wind. There are sun tanner and people parasailing above you. The smell of Jerk chicken permeates the air. The faint hint of ganja lingers. Vendors will be speaking loudly to sell their wares in their wonderful accents.

If you go on a snorkeling trip they take you a ways out from the beach to some fantastic coral reefs and here you will see everything you want to see in a snorkeling environment. It is like any other snorkeling experience with a beautiful reef, great looking fish and other wildlife existing.

If you want to get to other places on the island then you should find a reputable cab driver or use the guy who got you to and from the airport. You can also ask the owner of your hotel or the front desk clerk to find you a cab. Usually they know someone who will give you a fair price for your trip. At all-inclusive resorts they have people there who set up packages for the tourists and they are all reputable.

I have done a couple of excursions and can recommend a few. Rick's Café is in the cliffs and is a place owned by an American. Everyone goes to Rick's, just like in Casablanca. They go there for the food, the atmosphere, the music, the cliff diving (you can dive off the cliffs, or jump off them yourself if you choose), and the sunsets. It is a big tourist trap but it is so worth it. You will enjoy yourself at Ricks.

I also loved YS Falls. It is a bit of a ride to get to the falls from Negril (a couple of hours, I think) but when you get there it is like you are in another world. You can get a tour of the walk up the falls and up the river, and the guides only work for tips. The tour is a lot of fun, the water is cold and very refreshing, and the falls are stunning. You will need to get your suntan lotion there, and it will be expensive, because they want you to wear stuff that is environmentally friendly. The trip into the mountains is worth it because it shows you another side of Jamaica.

I have been to the Black River and that was fun and interesting. While there you will travel down the river in a small boat and see American crocodiles and other exotic wildlife. The pace is absolutely serene and the scenery is beautiful.

I have also been to Appleton Estate and I liked that as well. It is a working rum producer so there will be some heavy smells there, but it is a nice tour. They have a full gift shop that sells any kind of Appleton Rum you can imagine.

The best part of Negril, though, is the beach. Whether you are on Seven Mile Beach or Bloody Bay, the water is that beautiful Caribbean blue, turquoise, and green. The water is warm. The sound of people playing is so relaxing. The sun is bright and hot and by the end of the day you will be tired in a good way. When the sun sets there is nothing like it. You will go out to the beach every night to see the sun hit the waterline and fall off your plane of view and sometimes a moment before it disappears below the horizon, you may see a green sunset. It happens in a flash but it is something I have never seen anywhere else.

After the sun sets you most likely will go to your room and shower. At least that was what a large group of us always did when we finished our day at the beach. We would shower and then go off along the beach in search of dinner. There are places all up and down the beach. The night brings much fewer people to the beach but there will still be people out there trying to sell you souvenirs or drugs. As during the day, just tell them no, you are not interested. I would recommend at night you travel the beach at least in pairs to be safe. I have never had any trouble there and I do not know of anyone who has ever had trouble at night on the beach, but it is better to stay safe on your vacation.

Negril is what you make it. If you are looking for the perfect beach then Negril is for you. If you are looking for perfection in accommodations, then be sure to pick out a place that is expensive and that has high ratings. This book is a starting point in some ways. I have listed all the hotels, cottages, villas, etc. that are known to me. I have updated the book so all the names, the phone numbers, the web sites, and emails, are current. These reviews will give you an idea of how big the place is, how other people have rated the hotel or villa, and what type of amenities are available. When you hone in on a few places go look on the internet to see what other real travelers are saying about the place. Most people publish pictures of their rooms and the views from their hotels so it is easy to get a feel for the place even when you are thousands of miles away.

Negril isn't for everyone. It has a rustic feel and a back-to-nature kind of vibe. You will get asked to buy things every single day you are on the beach unless you stay at an all-inclusive on Bloody Bay. The big all-inclusive resorts do a good job of keeping the sellers away from you. The big all-inclusives do not give you a feel for the "real" Jamaica, but they are very nice. By that I mean, if you could lift the resort out of the earth and place it on another beach anywhere in the world, you most likely would not know the difference from one all-inclusive to another. The beach is the same but the experience is not. That is not to say that one is better than the other but different people like different things.

I like the places that are between rustic and the all-inclusives. Our friends stayed at a villa one year but we did not stay with them, we stayed next door. Their rooms were beautiful and up to any American standards, but during the day they always came to our beach because it was nicer. The beach was the almost same (ours was deeper and had more shade), and everything else was the same, they just paid about $500 more in a week to stay in a "nicer" place. I would not take that tradeoff because I like spending my money on other things.

So if you choose to go to Negril you have plenty of options. I have tried to give you information about all the places you can stay, a lot of different places you can eat, and a list of things to do. This is a starting point. I have discovered that Negril attracts a lot of people who come back year after year. Some people stay in the same place year in and year out, and some people stay at different places each year. I have found that the Jamaican people that you deal with on a day to day basis are some of the nicest, friendliest and welcoming people on earth. They are proud of Jamaica and proud of Negril.

Places to Eat

There are many different options when it comes to dining in Negril. There are so many different places to eat that I cannot possibly fit them all in this book. Some of the best places I have eaten at I have stumbled upon by accident. Do not be afraid to explore and challenge your palate. There are places to eat that are only a shack on the beach and there are some very elegant places that overlook the ocean on the Cliffs of Negril. There is even a Burger King in town. If you are really craving American food you can always go to Margaritaville, but I would do that only as a last resort; there are too many other good places to eat that only exist in Negril.

The following is simply a list of places that I have found or researched and are nice dining places. I also have been given some suggestions by readers. I will give all the information I have on location and phone numbers, but since some of the places are literally a hut on the beach, the only way to find some of these place is to get great directions. Some of the best food I have had in Jamaica has come from the roadside BBQs that are everywhere in Negril. If there is a web site I have included the link in the name and below it as well as other contact information.

When you are sitting on the beach relaxing, there will be people going up and down the beach selling food items. I have purchased and consumed fresh squeezed juices, fresh fruit from a woman called mama, patties for lunch (which are three patties for $5.00 and come in three different flavors), and I have heard there is an ice cream man who walks the beach selling fabulous rum raisin ice cream. There is really no need to leave the beach for most meals if that is your desire during the day. At night there are no food vendors walking the beach so you have to venture out if you want to go out to eat.

You will not go hungry in Negril and you will discover foods that are rich with flavor and seeped in Jamaican tradition.

Restaurants on Seven Mile Beach

Best in the West

Web Site: none

Phone: none

Email: none

Location: Across the street from Seven Mile Beach, across the street from the CocoLaPalm.

This is the kind of place I really enjoy. It is a divvy little tent across the street from Seven Mile Beach. They have a tent, a few tables and a bar and some fantastic jerk chicken. It is a place that could be on "Diners, Drive-ins and Dives" and it has great food and a regular clientele.

Chances Pizza Bar

https://www.facebook.com/pages/Chances-Negril/181899128534261

Phone: 876-532-9133

Email: none

Location: Next to Moon Dance Villas on Seven Mile Beach.

If you have kids or simply craving pizza, this is the place to go when in Negril. The pizza is done right, the toppings plentiful and the taste is very good. Expect to pay more than you would pay for a Pizza Hut pizza in the states but the quality is better than that anyway. I loved this place because the food tasted great and I like when pizza is done right.

Coletta's

Web Site: none

Phone: none

Email: none

Location: Across the street from the beach and opposite Rooms on the Beach.

Coletta's is an Authentic Jamaican restaurant where a lot of locals eat. I have never been there but I will be going the next time I am in Jamaica. The reviews are all outstanding and it sounds like the place is a hole-in-the-wall. The prices are very low and the food is homemade from scratch. This is a place where real Jamaican's eat.

Kenny's Jerk Chicken

Web Site: none

Phone: none

Email: none

Location: Right in front of the Times Square Mall, on the street.

OK, there is no place named Kenny's. We named this place Kenny's after the Seinfeld episode where Kramer was addicted to Kenny Rogers' chicken. We discovered this BBQ place on our first visit to Negril and we have never been disappointed. "Kenny" is located right on the roadside in front of the Times Square mall. All they serve is Jerk Chicken. We have had other Jerk Chicken but this one is the best by far according to my tastes.

Kuyaba Negril

http://www.kuyaba.com/restaurant1.htm

Phone: 876-957-4318

Email: kuyaba@cwjamaica.com

Location: On the beach across from Times Square Shopping center and next to Legends Resort.

We eat here on every trip we make to Negril. It is perfect for romantic dinners or fancy dinners with couples. The food is good, the prices fair, and the restaurant itself is beautiful. The service has always been good and it feels like a place you would go to on an anniversary or birthday.

Margaritaville Negril

http://www.margaritavillecaribbean.com/welcome_negril.html

Phone: 876-957-4467

Email: Form on the website

Location: Next to the Beach Comber Club on Seven Mile Beach.

It is almost a cliché, and it is also the name of a Jimmy Buffet song. It is also a tourist trap as well as a chain, but the atmosphere is fun, the food is decent if you are really craving American food, and the location is in the center of Seven Mile Beach. It will make you feel like you are back at home.

Niah's Patties

Web Site: none

Phone: none

Email: none

Figure 4 Niah's Patties

Location: Next to Lazy Dayz, on the beach, in an open lot that also sells beach towels and other tourist goods.

Niah's Patties is a shack on Seven Mile Beach. It is towards the Northern end of the beach right next to Lazy Dayz in an open lot that also sells a lot of towels and other tourist goods. Niah's makes everything fresh right in front of you, while you wait. The patties on the beach are pretty good, but these are fantastic. It is comparing hamburger to a New York Strip. They are more expensive than the patties on the beach. You can get Niah's patties stuffed with many different options from hamburger to lobster, from Italian to curry chicken. The patties are huge and relatively inexpensive. Buy or bring a beer and eat at one of the picnic tables provided. I think we paid about $10 a patty.

This is one place I never miss going to when I am in Negril.

Sun Beach

http://www.facebook.com/pages/Sun-Beach-bar-Negril/282440475118065

Phone: 876-957-9118

Email: None

Location: Near the Fire Fly, the For Real and the Coco La Palm hotels right in the sand on Seven Mile Beach.

A little place that is right on the beach. The food tastes fantastic and the atmosphere cannot be beat except maybe at the Rock House. Besides all that, the prices are very reasonable. Get there for dinner and watch the sunset as you dine.

Restaurants on the Cliffs or West End

The Cliffs is sometimes called the West End. It is a short cab ride from Seven Mile Beach and but it would be a long and dangerous walk if you tried to walk there. The road is only two lanes wide and there is no sidewalk or a place for pedestrians. It has a different feel than Seven Mile Beach and there are a bunch of hotels and resorts up in the cliffs. It is fun to get away for a bit even if it is just a few miles down the road!

3 Dives Restaurant

http://www.maherconsulting.com/3dives/

Phone: 876-782-9990

876-472-5457

Email: none

Location: The Cliffs of Negril.

3 Dives Restaurant is a classic Jamaican dining experience that overlooks the ocean on the Cliffs in Negril. You do not need to dress up in your fancy clothes, the food is absolutely authentic and tastes great, and the attitude there is pure Jamaica where you go there for the great views, the good vibes at very reasonable prices. Call ahead for reservations and get a seat next to the ocean and sit back, eat a little jerk chicken and watch the sun set on another glorious day in Jamaica.

The Blue Mahoe Restaurant (located at The Spa Retreat Boutique Hotel)

http://www.thespajamaica.com/cm1.cfm?fid=4&lang=1&html=dining.html

Phone: 855-843-7725 (US and Canada)

876-957-4329

Email: rsvp@thespajamaica.com

Location: The Cliffs of Negril.

One of the most elegant restaurants in Negril and located at the Spa Retreat Hotel on the Cliffs of Negril. The restaurant has everything you would expect from a fancy and high-end place to eat. It has stunning food, incredible views and all of it is done in very elegant surroundings. Cloth table clothes and crystal stemware makes it the kind of place you would visit for special occasions when you want to dress up and hit the town.

The Canoe Bar

http://www.realnegril.com/canoe/

Phone: 876-878-5893

Email: canoebeachbar@gmail.com

Location: On the last piece of beach right before the Cliffs of Negril.

A beautiful little shack right on the beach overlooking the ocean awaits you when you go to the Canoe Bar. This place feels like Negril and the prices are very moderate. Thursday night they have live music and $3.00 Red Stripes to enhance your dining experience.

Ciao Jamaica

http://www.ciaojamaica.com/

Phone: 876-957-4395

Email: eat@ciaojamaica.com

Location: The Cliffs of Negril.

Are you craving Italian food in Jamaica? Not every restaurant severs only Jamaican food. Ciao Jamaica is a very family friendly place that even has a children's menu and serves Italian food as well as Jamaican dishes. If you are craving a lobster pizza then this is your place. The cost is about the same you would pay at a decent restaurant in the United States. A very lovely place with ocean and sunset views and good food and they will even pick you up at your hotel and drop you off for free!

Catch a Falling Star Resort (Ivan's Bar and Restaurant)

http://www.catchajamaica.com/ivans.htm

Phone: 876-957-0390

Email: stay@catchajamaica.com

Location: The Cliffs of Negril.

Ivan's is a very nice and fancy restaurant that has the same atmosphere as the Rock House Resort. It has sweeping views of the ocean and can be very romantic. Sunsets are stunning and the food is quite nice. Expect elegant dinners by candlelight at night and at sunset.

Just Natural

Web Site: none

Phone: 876-957-0235

Email: none

Location: The Cliffs of Negril.

Just Natural is Negril's vegetarian and seafood destination. The food is fresh and there is no meat on the menu. They are known for their French toast breakfast and fresh fish. I have never eaten here but I have heard it is nice.

Presley's Bar and Grill

Web Site: none

Phone: 876-440-9833

Email: none

Location: The Cliffs of Negril.

Presley's is a very unique seafood restaurant located in the cliffs of Negril. You have to call the morning you want to eat dinner for a reservation and at the same time you tell the chef what you want for dinner. They will go out and catch your dinner for you the same day of your dinner reservations. If it is not lobster season you will be out of luck if you want lobster. The food is extremely fresh, well-loved and a bit pricier than most Negril restaurants but you get what you pay for. It is another cozy little shack with a bar and tables and a chef with amazing talents cooking your food.

Rock House Resort on the Cliffs

http://www.rockhousehotel.com/eat

Phone: 876-957-4373

Email: info@rockhousehotel.com

Location: The Cliffs of Negril.

The Rock House Resort has some of the most exceptional views anywhere in Jamaica. There are tables that sit along the cliff and overlook the ocean and you can't beat the view. The food is upscale for Jamaica and is very tasty. This is the perfect place to take your wife or significant other for a special night on the town. You can call The Rock House and get a free ride to the resort, but you are on your own to get a cab to get back to Seven Mile Beach. If you email or call ahead you can get the most romantic table in the place, one that sits all alone about 40 feet away from the rest of the restaurant, out on the cliffs. This table only seats four people at the most but it is designed for two.

Restaurants in the Town of Negril

Burger King

Web Site: none

Phone: none

Location: In the town of Negril.

Burger King is the only fast food chain I know of in Negril. Montego Bay has all of the big fast food places but once you leave that big city you are out of luck if you want fast food. Burger King is located right when you enter the town of Negril. There is no way you will miss it.

Sweet Spice Restaurant

Web Site: none

Phone: 876-957-4621

Location: In the town of Negril.

Sweet Spice is a restaurant one of my readers told me about (thank you Bill!). It is an authentic Jamaican restaurant that is favored by the locals. It is inexpensive and has great food in a very relaxed atmosphere and a lot of the locals will point you here when you ask for authentic Jamaican food.

Xtabi

Web Site: http://www.xtabi-negril.com/restaurant.html

Phone: 876-957-0121

876-957-0524

Location: Near Negril's West end, near the center of town

Xtabi has great food and an upscale feel. Tremendous seafood options await you as well as other traditional Jamaican food like Jerk Chicken or Conch. Located in the Xtabi hotel the restaurant is more than a shack on the beach the food is a bit pricier than other places but worth it for a special night out.

Things to Do in and Around Negril

If you get tired of sitting on the beach all day drinking a beer or two and just relaxing, then there are other attractions in and around Negril that will keep you busy for the day. Some of these are geared towards nature lovers and some are geared towards having more fun. Either way you can talk to a taxi driver and they will give you a price of what it would cost for them to take you to these attractions or you can ask for help at your hotel; most places know a guy. Some of these attractions will take a significant amount of driving and will eat into your day. If this is the case then plan ahead and make sure you will have enough time that day to fit in the trip. Jamaica is a very beautiful tropical island and there are many more things to do than to lie on the beach all day.

Blue Hole Mineral Springs

http://www.blueholejamaica.com/

Phone: 876-860-8805

Email: matt@blueholejamaica.com

Located about 25 minutes southeast of Negril this is a natural mineral spring located in limestone. People that have been there absolutely love it and go there again and again. Besides the huge pool located in a limestone hole, there are other activities like horseback riding, music, Jamaican food, a swimming pool and bar, and volleyball. Blue Hole is family friendly and very relaxing. Where else can you go and spend the day for about $10 (that is the entrance fee only. Food and beer are extra)?

Kool Runnings Water Park

http://www.koolrunnings.com/

Phone: 876-957-5400

Email: info@koolrunnings.com

Kool Runnings Water Park is an attraction with 10 water slides, (mostly closed slides/tubes) as well as an interactive children's play area for toddlers. There are three themed restaurants as well as go-karts, bungee trampolines and a carousel. It is across the highway from Seven Mile Beach but it is further North up the coast, so for most resorts you might be better off getting a cab to take you there. The park is open 11 AM to 7 PM daily, Tuesday through Sunday.

YS Falls

http://www.ysfalls.com/

Phone: 876-997-6360

Email: ysfalls@cwjamaica.com

Figure 5 YS Falls

YS-Falls is located 50 miles east of Negril, although the roads wind through the mountains so it takes a couple of hours to get there from Negril by car. When my wife and I went to YS falls we also went to Appleton Estates for a tour and to the Black River. All three are near each other, relatively speaking. At YS falls you can walk up the YS River and there are nine different levels of waterfalls. You can also ride a zip line or go into a natural spring pool. It is very eco-friendly and you have to buy the sunscreen from them because it does not hurt the environment. We had a guide on our trip and he stayed with us until we were completely at the head of the falls. If you get a guide they work on tips only and they usually take a large group. The river and falls are absolutely amazing and refreshing.

Appleton Estates

http://us.appletonestate.com/

Phone: none

Email: Form on website

Appleton Estates is the oldest and most famous of all of Jamaica's sugar estates and rum makers. It is nestled in the Nassau Valley on either side of the Black River in the Southwest of Jamaica. You can take a tour here to see how they make the rum. It is an interactive tour and they will show you how they pressed sugar cane before machines were invented to do it (in fact they had me playing the part of the mule, turning the gears). The visitor's center is modern and well-equipped and at the end of your tour they have every kind of Appleton's rum they make for sale.

Black River Tours

Web Site: none

Phone: none

Email: none

There are several different companies that provide tours on the Black River. If you are so inclined you can hire a driver that will take you to the Black River, YS Falls and Appleton's for the rum tour. All three places are near each other and are about a two hour drive from Negril. You can easily fit all three places in one day and it is fun. The Black River is beautiful and it has American Crocodiles that live in it. They all have names given to them by the boat drivers and they are "tame" enough to eat chicken out of the driver's hands. You will get a close up view of nature and the trip takes about 1 ½ hours to complete.

Rick's Café

http://www.rickscafejamaica.com/

Phone: 876-957-0380

Email: info@rickscafejamaica.com

Figure 6 Sunset at Rick's Cafe, Negril

Rick's is the ultimate tourist place in Negril. It was opened many years ago by an American and is located on the cliffs in Negril. It is about a 15 minute cab ride from Seven Mile Beach. Rick's is known for their sunsets so the busiest, and most fun time to go there, is late afternoon where you would stay for dinner and watch the sunset. If you are brave bring a swimsuit and jump off the very high cliffs. If you are not so brave watch the professionals and other amateurs do it. There is always a band there.

They have very decent American food and a nice gift shop. Yes, it is touristy, but it is also a must see location.

Dolphin Cove

http://negril.dolphincoveja.com/

Phone: 876-974-5335

Email: inquiry@onestopva.com

Dolphin Cove is located 45 minutes from Negril or Montego Bay in Lucea, Jamaica. This facility is the largest in the Western Hemisphere on 23 acres and features a large natural lagoon enclosure for the 8 Bottleneck Dolphins on site. Swim with the dolphins in Jamaica!

Canopy Tour

http://www.canopytour.com/montegobay.html

Phone: 305-433-2241 (US number)

Email: info@canopytours.com

This attraction in located in Montego Bay and consists of a series of decks and platforms mounted in the trees of the forest. You zip line from platform to platform. There is a weight restriction of 265 lbs. and being able to ride on this line also requires a body-type that will fit in the equipment. I think this means that if you are 4'6" and weigh 265, odds are you will not fit in the equipment. If you are addicted to an adrenaline rush then this is the attraction for you. Explore the Jamaican wildlife over the tops of the trees and through the forest.

Mayfield Falls

http://www.mayfieldfalls.com/

Phone: 876-610-8612

876-792-2074

Email: info@mayfieldfalls.com

About a one hour drive from Negril, Mayfield Falls is located in the Dolphin Head Mountains in Glenbrook. Mayfield Falls offers mini-waterfalls and numerous pools, for swimming, diving, Jacuzzi type massages, and more. It is very much a wet and active tour.

Admission is about $20 per person. Bring water shoes (they do rent them there but they are about $7 a pair) because you will be walking on rocky terrain. The experience might be too much for the very young or the very old; there is a bit of physicality needed when you go here. It will cost about $120 to get a cab ride there and when you are done you should tip the guides and photographer.

Things you can do by hiring people on the beach.

Besides finding things to do far afield from Negril, there are many things you can do right on the beach. All of the things listed below can be purchased from and start and end on the beach. You can negotiate the price on anything in Jamaica, and the options listed below are no different.

I made comments on the things I have done while in Negril. There may be more things to do but I think I have most of it covered.

Bonfires: Some hotels will have a bonfire at night after sunset. While walking the beach look for a pile of wood stacked like a teepee that stands about 12 feet tall. Hotels and bars do this to attract drinkers at night.

Catamaran tour with a lobster lunch: This was one of the best deals in Negril. For $40 US we were given all the beer or rum punches we could drink, snorkeling out by the reef off the beach (you snorkel early in the drinking process so you will not drown), a catamaran ride to a different island, and a lobster tail lunch. The tickets can be bought in front of the Boat Bar and the tours leave in the morning and you will not get back until the afternoon. Beware, when we were on the island four people from Hedonism showed up in a canoe and they did not have a stitch of clothing between them …nudity that day was not uncommon.

Deep Sea Fishing

Glass Bottom Boat Tour: In front of Coco LaPalms hotel. You will get a better rate if you walk up to the boat and ask for pricing there.

Horseback Riding

Jet Skis

Massages: Most of the bigger all-inclusive hotels have masseuses on staff and they are about $100/hour. If you get a massage from a woman on the beach the equipment might not be what you are used to but the massage itself is wonderful and it is about half the price.

Parasailing

Reggae Concerts: These concerts are put on by various hotels on different days of the week. You will see people walking up and down the beach with megaphones advertising the concerts that are happening that week. They always feature a reggae superstar, according to the hype. I have been to a few concerts and have enjoyed myself at each one of them.

SCUBA Diving: For this activity you must be certified. There are SCUBA centers on the beach that will give you SCUBA lessons, but be forewarned that the cost is easily a few hundred dollars.

Snorkeling

Walking: There is nothing better than a long walk on the beach with the waves crashing beside you. The walks can be romantic or they can be your exercise for the day to work off all the Red Stripes you will consume.

Where to Stay

Negril has options when it comes on places to stay. What started out as a funky little beach town that only a few people travelled to, has now become a funky little beach town that also caters to the well-healed traveler. This means that there are many hotels, motels, cottages, villas, or condo options available in Negril. Negril can accommodate the needs and desires of most any traveler. There is even a resort where you can be completely nude.

Besides some of the all-inclusive resorts, there are not any big name hotel chains that have places in Negril. That is a big part of the charm that is Negril. When you go there it is like stepping back in time. You will find a lot of places that are family owned and run. People who visit Negril tend to stay at the same places year after year, and they use the same drivers year after year.

The type of places to stay in Jamaica falls into three or four different categories but these categories are not written in stone. The first is the all-inclusive resorts, which are usually very modern and up to hotel standards anywhere in the world. If you stay at an all-inclusive resort your every want and desire in regards to food and alcohol are paid for in advance and you will not need to worry about bringing extra money along on your trip and you will not have to worry where your next meal will be eaten. These are the only hotel chains in Negril.

The next level is the condos and villas. These places usually have a refrigerator and stove in them allowing you to cut down on your meal expenses. Some come with maid service where there will be someone there to cook and clean for you. The villas tend to be very much up to American standards while the condos sometimes tend towards being older and in need of some paint and TLC.

The third level consists of places that are like any other mid-level hotel you will find in the United States. These are basic hotel rooms with few amenities and they are usually nothing to brag about to friends or co-workers. The reason to be in Jamaica is for the water, sand and culture, so who really cares about your room, right? That is why so many hotels listed below have high ratings, because the attraction is the beach and not the hotel.

Finally, there are the cottages. The cottages are family run and have been around for decades. Rooms tend to have their own vibe and no two rooms are alike. These places are rustic and are the ideal no-stress get away and in many ways represent what Negril was 20 or 30 years ago (or so I am told).

When you get a room there are some things to consider. Negril is a safe place that you will feel comfortable at almost all the time. That being said, there is petty crime if you give people the opportunity. Do not leave things like money or computers just lying around. Most places have room safes that you can use but they usually charge an additional fee (usually $3.00 a day) and a deposit for the key. I have found that the people you interact with the most, the people that work at the hotels, are polite and honest. I personally have never had anything stolen or gone missing while staying in Negril. The people I have travelled with have not experienced any theft either. Simply take normal precautions you would take anywhere else in the world and you will be fine.

I also stay at places that have security. I have found if you stay at places where people are monitored going in and out, that you tend not to have things stolen from your room. Almost every place in Negril has a guard.

Bloody Bay is where all of the bigger hotels or all-inclusives are located. There are only four resorts on Bloody Bay and one across the street. Each resort here is a couple hundred rooms big. Bloody Bay is nice and there are not a lot of people on the beach trying to sell you things.

The resorts that are not on Seven Mile Beach, but are across the street, tend to be the more rustic places. There are a few exceptions so read the description of the place first. The places that are NOT on the beach are cheaper than a comparative place that is on the beach. This is common sense. Norman Manley Boulevard is the name of the street that bisects the beach from the "garden" resorts. It is a fairly busy road but there is also ample opportunity to cross the street safely. Traffic moves fast on this road and people drive on the left like in the UK. Be sure to look in the correct direction before you cross the street.

Seven Mile Beach is an eclectic assortment of different hotel types. You will be able to find a place that you are comfortable with without any problems. Decide what type of place you want to stay, decide how much you can afford, and take the plunge!

Map of Hotels on Seven Mile Beach, Negril Jamaica

This is a word map representation of the hotels on Seven Mile beach in Negril, Jamaica. The top of this list is north and the hotels exist in Jamaica in the same order that they appear on the list. Places to eat are indicated by bold lettering and one star. The items underlined and with stars at the beginning and end of the name are across the street from Seven Mile Beach, but still great places to stay.

 **North**

Map Key

"*" **and bold and indented**   = Restaurants

****name****   = Hotels on the other side of the road from the beach

"$$"   = ATM's

Top Horizontal Line   = Jetty separating Bloody Beach and Seven Mile Beach

Bloody Bay

Club RIU Negril All-Inclusive

*Sunset at the Palms Bar and Grill

****Sunset At the Palms****

RIU Palace Tropical Bay All-Inclusive

Couples Negril

****Fed-Ex/ATM $$****

Grand Lido Resort All-Inclusive

****Craft Market/ATM $$****

Seven Mile Beach

Carib Beach Apartments

Hedonism II All-Inclusive

Sandals Negril Beach Resort All-Inclusive

Our Past Time Villas

Azul Sensatori Jamaica, by Karisma (formerly Beaches Sandy Bay)

****Kool Runnings Water Park****

Negril Villa

   *Cosmos Restaurant

Beaches Negril Resort

Couples Swept Away

Top Beach Cabins Rooms and Bar

Foote Prints Hotel

****Small Grocery Store****

Sea Wind Resort

    *Conch Hill Restaurant

    *Pilot's Cafe

Negril Palms Resort, The

Donaldson's Inn

Sea Sand Echo Villas

Sea Splash Resort

Doris Rooms

Negril Tree House

Country - Country

Crystal Waters Villas

    *Margaritaville

Beachcomber Club

    *Chances Restaurant

Sunqest Cottages (Formerly Wild Parrot Beach Cottages)

Firefly Cottages

Secrets Cabins

****Rayon Hotel****

    *Sunbeach Bar & Restaurant

Sandy Haven

****Greenleaf Cabins and Devon House****

****The Golden Sunset Villas****

CocoLaPalm

Idle Awhile

****Calalloo Butik****

Charela Inn

****Moonrise Villas****

 *Rainbow Arch Restaurant

****Sea Breeze Apartments****

White Sands

Nirvana

Lazy Dayz

Gatehouse Villa

 *Niah's Patties

Mariposa Hideaway

****Freedom Villa****

 *Boat Bar and Restaurant

****Tropical Fantasy****

Rondel Village

Whistling Bird

Fun Holiday Beach Resort

Aqua Negril Resort

Roots Bamboo

****Villa Mora****

Rooms on the Beach

****Jah B's Doll House Cottages****

Valentine Villas @ Trombone's Place

****Coletta's****

    *23/7 Bar (New Nation Restaurant)

****Classique Cottages****

    *Arthur's Beach Bar

Alfred's

Grand Pineapple Resort All-Inclusive

****Lily Mae's Guest House****

Caribbean Delight

Merril's I All-Inclusive

****Hidden Paradise****

    *Mama Flo's

    * 1 Mile Cookshop

Merril's II All-Inclusive

Yellow Bird

Merril's III All-Inclusive

****BT Cottages****

    *Risky Business

Jamaica Tamboo Resort

****Legends****

Legends

Kuyaba Negril

****Pure Garden Resort (formerly the Bungalo)****

Bourbon Beach

****Perseverance****

Bar-B-Barn Cottages

Mom's Place

****Sunrise Club****

*Reggae Man Café (24 hours)**

****Coral Seas Garden Motel****

Coconuts International

*Willowood**

Beach House Villas

Negril Beach Club (Mariner's Negril Beach Club)

Errol's Sunset Café and Rooms

Travelers Hotel Beach Resort

Shields Negril Villas

****Yoga Center****

Ansell's Thatch Walk Cottages

Sunset on the Beach Hotel

The Town of Negril

*Burger King**

$$ Scotia Bank ATM $$

Drug Stores

Hi-Lo

Hotels, Hostels, Villas, Cottages, and Cabins on Seven Mile Beach, Negril

Figure 7 The Negril Beach Club

I have put together the most comprehensive list of hotels, villas, hostels, cottages, and apartments available to rent in Negril Jamaica on Seven Mile Beach. The list is alphabetical, and below the first section is a section that has website information, email addresses if available, and phone numbers to make reservations. I have also included a list of amenities available at each location as well as the number of rooms on the property. I did not include pricing on these listings because there are usually two different pricing structures for summer and winter and the prices could change at any time. You will pay less money for more rustic accommodations.

The general rule is that the All-Inclusives will be the most expensive option because all of your food, drinks and round trip transportation (for some) are included. The villas would be the second most expensive option and for a large villa the cost for the room alone could be more than the all-inclusives, but you can usually fit a few couples in each villa so that brings the prices down. The rest of the rooms on Seven Mile Beach fall somewhere in the middle for cost and the rooms that are across the highway from the beach are usually the cheapest.

I have included ratings of each of these places based on the reviews on a few different web sites. These are just general guidelines. You will notice that there really are no two ratings and very few three ratings (out of five). This is probably because it does not matter where you stay in Negril because you will be on one of the most beautiful beaches in the world and your problems tend to slip away. People tend to understand what type of place they are staying at and that is taken into consideration when they rate the place.

Keep in mind also that the all-inclusives tend to be up to American standards when it comes to the luxury and quality of the buildings. They are catering to an upscale market. A lot of the villas are also constructed very well and would be up to a top-tier American hotel. That being said a lot of the rooms listed below will be more rustic than you are used to seeing. They will have wires that are not buried in the walls, bathrooms that look a little worse for wear, the appliances might be older and well-worn, and the beds will not be the best you have ever experienced. Even with all of the above mentioned items every place I have stayed at, the maids were very good about cleaning the rooms and cleaning the bedding. I have never been wary of a room I have rented in Negril.

My personal preference is to find a place that at least has a refrigerator and a safe. A lot of hotel desks will keep your valuables locked up for you as well. If you have a refrigerator you can buy beer and keep it cold, have refrigerated food items and snacks, and odds are you will be able to make ice. Pack a collapsible portable cooler as well as a re-freezable ice pack so you can take more than one drink down to the beach and keep them cold in the hot Jamaican sun.

To see a mapped layout of the hotels on the beach, please see the section title "Map of Hotels on Seven Mile Beach Negril, Jamaica," in the previous chapter.

Finally, the all-inclusives are denoted with an asterisk before the name. The hotels on the other side of the highway, not on the beach, are noted with three asterisks and are in bold type.

Hotels Listed Alphabetically.

Figure 8 Travelers Hotel Beach Resort

Key:

*and bold = All-Inclusive

**** = Across the street from Seven Mile Beach

Alfred's

Ansell's Thatch Walk Cottages

Aqua Negril Resort

Azul Sensatori Jamaica, by Karisma (formerly Beaches Sandy Bay)

Bar-B-Barn Cottages

Beach House Villas

Beachcomber Club

*Beaches Negril Resort (Sandals) All-Inclusive

Bourbon Beach

BT Cottages

Carib Beach Apartments

Caribbean Delight

Charela Inn

****Chippewa Village Negril Hotel ****

****Classique Cottages (formerly Shamrock Classique Cottages)****

*Club RIU Negril All-Inclusive

CocoLaPalm

****Coral Seas Garden Motel****

Country - Country

*Couples Negril All-Inclusive

Couples Swept Away

Crystal Waters Villas

Donaldson's Inn

Doris Rooms

Errol's Sunset Café and Rooms

Firefly Cottages

Foote Prints Hotel

****Freedom Villa****

Fun Holiday Beach Resort

****Gardenia Resort****

Gatehouse Villa

****The Golden Sunset Villas****

*Grand Lido Resort All-Inclusive

*Grand Pineapple Resort All-Inclusive

****Greenleaf Cabins and Devon House****

*Hedonism II All-Inclusive and Adult Only

****Hidden Paradise****

Idle Awhile

****Jah B's Doll House Cottages****

Jamaica Tamboo Resort

Kuyaba Negril

Lazy Dayz

Legends

****Lily Mae's Guest House****

Mariposa Hideaway

*Merril's I

*Merril's II

*Merril's III

Mom's Place

Moonrise Villas

Negril Beach Club (Mariner's Negril Beach Club)

Negril Palms Resort, The

Negril Tree House

Negril Villa

Nirvana

****Ocean View Villa****

Our Past Time Villas

****Perseverance****

****Pure Garden Resort****

****Rayon Hotel****

*RIU Palace Tropical Bay All-Inclusive

****Rondel Village****

Rooms on the Beach

Roots Bamboo

Sandals Negril beach Resort

Sandy Haven

Sea Sand Eco Villas

Sea Splash Resort

Sea Wind Resort

Secrets Cabins

Shields Negril Villas

Sunquest Cottages (Formerly Wild Parrot Beach Cottages)

****Sunrise Club****

****Sunset at the Palms****

Sunset on the Beach Hotel

Top Beach Cabins Rooms and Bar

Travelers Hotel Beach Resort

****Tropical Fantasy****

Valentine Villas @ Trombone's Place

****Villa Mora****

Whistling Bird

****White Sands****

Yellow Bird

****Yoga Center****

Hotels with Links to Web Pages and Contact Information Listed Alphabetically.

Amenities Key:

 = Restaurant    = Bar   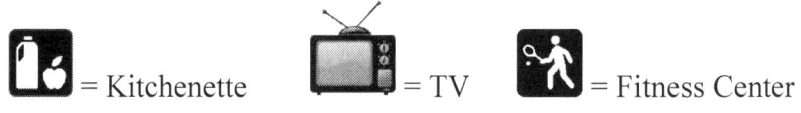 = Free Breakfast

= Kitchenette   = TV   = Fitness Center

= Wi-Fi Available   = Disabled Access

= Pool   = Rustic Accommodations

Hotels with Amenities List

Alfred's Ocean Palace 3.5 out of 5

http://www.alfreds.com/

Phone: 920-967-2119 (US)

      876-957-4669

Email: info@alfreds.com

Alfred's is a funky little place to stay that is safe, clean and simply has basic rooms with few modern amenities. It is located about in the middle of Seven Mile Beach. Live music happens on Tuesday, Friday and Sunday nights.

Ansell's Thatch Walk Cottages 3 out of 5

11 Rooms, some with kitchenettes

http://ansellsnegril.com/

Phone: 718-515-3399 (United States)

      876-957-3419 (Jamaica)

Email: Ansell4643@cs.com

Ansell's is an eclectic mix of rustic cabins along with beautiful and functional studio-type apartments.

Aqua Negril Resort 5 out of 5

6 Rooms

http://www.aquanegrilresort.com/

Phone: 876-957-9037

Email: aquanegril@yahoo.com

Aqua Negril is a boutique hotel in Negril located on Seven Mile Beach that offers free breakfast in the mornings.

Azul Sensatori Jamaica, by Karisma (formerly Beaches Sandy Bay) 5 out of 5

http://www.karismahotels.com/hotelsresorts/foreveryone/azulsensatorijamaica

Phone: 888-280-7558

Email: reservations@khrreservations.com

Karisma has opened their very first property on Negril's Seven Mile Beach and it is called the Azul Sensatori Jamaica, by Kirisma. It is a mouthful, to be sure. This property used to be Beaches on Sandy Bay, a property owned by Sandals.

Karisma owns luxury hotels in Mexico and elsewhere. When they purchased this resort they poured a significant amount of money into it to get it up to their very high standards. This is truly a world-class hotel and you do pay for the luxury and the service. The reviews have been absolutely outstanding and from what I have read of their other properties, this resort will cater to those who want to be pampered.

Bar-B-Barn Cottages 4 out of 5

30 Rooms

http://www.barbbarn.com/

Phone: 800-240-0189 (Toll Free US)

    876-957-4755

    876-957-4267

Email: Form on web site.

The Bar-B-Barn Cottages is a family run hotel that boasts most of the amenities found in your average-to-upscale hotel in the U.S. This hotel is more upscale than the word "cottages" indicates. Handicap accessible rooms are available upon request.

Beach House Villas 4.5 out of 5

21 Rooms

http://www.negriljamaicavillas.com/

Phone: 305-767-2596 (USA)

    800-471-6347 (USA Toll Free)

    0-808-234-1408 (UK Toll Free)

Email: contact@negriljamaicavillas.com

Beach House Villas is made up of villas, studio apartments and one bedroom apartments for rent. As the term "villas" implies, this is a high-end rental and is quite luxurious.

Beachcomber Club 3.5 out of 5

46 Rooms

http://www.beachcomberclub.com/

Phone: 877-713-8784

876-957-4170

Email: reservations@beachcomberclub.com

The Beachcomber Club consists of nice sized luxurious rooms, studio rooms, one bedroom, and two bedroom apartments. It has several nice amenities and is located almost in the middle of Seven Mile Beach.

Beaches Negril Resort All-Inclusive (Sandals) 5 out of 5

225 Rooms

http://www.beaches.com/main/ng/ng-home.cfm

Phone: 888-BEACHES (888-232-2437)

Email: Form on the website

Sandals owns both Beaches Negril and Beaches Sandy Bay and both sites are all-inclusive properties. When you stay at one resort you have access to both resorts for bars, pool and restaurants. There are multiple places to eat and drink and multiple pools, including a lazy river and water slides. If you love all-inclusives you will love both of these properties.

Bourbon Beach 3 out of 5

http://www.bbnegril.com/

Phone: 876-374-4982

Email: bbnegril@bbnegril.com

Kevin.Hughes@bbnegril.com

Bourbon Beach is a boutique hotel with rooms that each have two double beds. Each room can accommodate up to four people. Wi-Fi is available in public areas but reception is not good in the rooms.

BT's Resort Cottages 1 out of 5

24 Rooms if you include Perseverance

http://www.go-jam.com/perseverance-e.html

Phone: 876-957-4333

876-957-4744

Email: info@go-jam.com

BT's Resort is located across the street from Seven Mile Beach and is run with a resort called Perseverance. It is truly a rustic place to stay and room rates as of this writing start at $25 a night U.S. Bathrooms are either shared, outside or private. The more you pay the more privacy you get with the bathrooms. If you simply want a no-frills room cheap, this is the place for you.

Carib Beach Apartments 4 out of 5

2 Rooms

http://www.jamaicalink.com/carib/

Phone: 876-957-4358

876-957-9325

Email: carib@jamaicalink.com

These two condominiums are located right on the tip between Seven Mile Beach and Bloody Bay. There is a nude beach and a regular beach within a couple hundred yards of this complex, the nude beach is basically the same beach used as Hedonism. Firefly Cottages runs the rentals of these two units, so when you book a stay here you will have to get to Firefly Cottages first to get the room key. This is a very romantic location and the room rates are very reasonable. These units have full kitchens in both rooms.

Caribbean Delight No Ratings

No website

Phone: 876-422-0339

Email: caribbean.delight@yahoo.com

Caribbean Delight is a located on Seven Mile Beach and it one of the more rustic hotels or cottages on the beach. They have no web presence but you can either call or email them for information.

I saw one posting online that this hotel might be closed so I emailed the owner. They are indeed still open and can be contacted via phone or email.

Charela Inn 4.5 out of 5

47 Rooms

http://www.charela.com/

Phone: 876-957-4277

876-957-4648

876-957-4649

876-957-4650

Email: info@charela.com

Skype: charela.inn.hotel

The Charlea Inn is a very nice hotel where each room has either a patio or a balcony. The beach in front of Charlea has plenty of palm trees so there is always shade. The rooms are clean and very nice.

Chippewa Village Negril Hotel 4 out of 5

3 Rooms, 7 Suites

http://chippewavillageresort.com/

Phone: 876-957-4676

213-283-9232 (US and Canada)

Email: chippewavillage@hotmail.com

Chippewa Village a little family run hotel and is owned by an American. There are three rooms and seven suites but the place still has a little bit of that rustic Negril charm. There are three large dogs that live on this property and you should not stay here if you do not like dogs.

Classique Cottages (Formerly Shamrock Classique Cottages) Next to Shamrock Market) No ratings

9 Rooms

Web Site: none

Phone: 876-957-4696

Email: jondel2003@yahoo.com

Information about Classique Cottages is very hard to come by on the internet. The information provided is the most current and up-to-date as far as I know. This is one of the very rustic places across the street from Negril's Seven Mile Beach.

As of June 2014 I called and they are still open for business and the email address is valid!

Club RIU Negril All-Inclusive 4.5 out of 5

420 Rooms

http://www.riu.com/en/Paises/jamaica/negril/clubhotel-riu-negril/index.jsp

Phone: 888-RIU-4990 (US)

   866-845-3765 (Canada)

   0870-099-0935 (UK)

   876-957-5700

Email: clubhotel.negril@riu.com

The RIU hotels are both located on Bloody Bay which is connected to Seven Mile Beach at the North end of the beach. RIU hotels are all-inclusive and both have several different restaurants, bars and pool areas. When you stay at one you have privileges at the other's bars and restaurants.

CocoLaPalm 4 out of 5

75 Rooms

http://www.cocolapalm.com/

Phone: 800-320-8821 (Toll Free US)

   876-957-4227

Email: Form on website

CocoLa Palm is owned and run by people from my home state,

Minnesota. I have read so many nice things about this place, including a few reviews that said this is the nicest place to stay that is not all-inclusive. The rooms are very nice and the hospitality cannot be beat.

Coral Seas Beach (and Garden) Resorts **(It is also known as Sunset on the Beach) All-inclusive 4 out of 5**

32 Rooms for Beach Resort

26 Rooms, 2 Suites for Garden Resort

http://www.coralseasresort.com/

Phone: 876-957-9226

    888-790-5264 (Toll free US)

    0-800-7297-2900 (Toll free UK)

Email: reservations@coralseasresort.com

The Coral Seas consists of two different hotels, the Coral Seas Beach (also known as Sunset Beach) and the Coral Seas Garden. The Coral Seas Beach is located on Seven Mile Beach, near the town of Negril, while the Coral Seas Garden is located across the street from the beach further to the north. When you reserve rooms here the transportation from the airport is included and is in a very nice limousine.

Country Country 3.5 out of 5

20 Rooms

http://countrynegril.com/

Phone: 888-689-2021

876-957-4273

Email: countrynegril@gmail.com

Country Country is at the upper end of cottages you can rent in Negril. It is located a few doors down from Margaritaville and towards the middle of Seven Mile Beach. If you want a cottage experience but also want luxury, this is the place for you. Relax your cares away at this little Negril gem.

Couples Negril All-Inclusive Resort 5 out of 5

234 Rooms

http://couples.com/negril/

Phone: 800-268-7537 (US Toll Free)

+44-1582-794-420 (UK)

876-957-5960

Email: Form on website

Couples Negril, along with Couple Swept away, are two of the more expensive all-inclusive resorts you can stay at while in Jamaica. With the higher price comes a lot of extras included in the cost that you would have to pay for at most all other all-inclusives. The things you can do for no cost at this resort include unlimited golf, SBUBA diving, Dunn's River Falls tour, a catamaran cruise, water skiing, reef snorkeling, etc. You truly get what you pay for in upgrades. Like other all-inclusives there are several bars and pools to choose from. This all-inclusive also includes free transportation to and from the airport.

Couples Swept Away All-Inclusive Resort 5 out of 5

http://couples.com/swept-away/

Phone: 800-268-7537 (US Toll Free)

+44-1582-794-420 (UK)

876-957-4061

Email: Form on website

Couples Swept Away, along with Couples Negril, are two of the more expensive all-inclusive resorts you can stay at while in Jamaica. With the higher price comes a lot of extras included in the cost that you would have to pay for at most all other all-inclusives. The things you can do for no cost at this resort include unlimited golf, SBUBA diving, Dunn's River Falls tour, a catamaran cruise, water skiing, reef snorkeling, etc. You truly get what you pay for in upgrades. Like other all-inclusives there are several bars and pools to choose from. This all-inclusive also includes free transportation to and from the airport.

Crystal Waters Villas 5 out of 5

10 Rooms

http://www.crystalwaters.net/

Phone: 876-957-4284

Email: crystalwaters@cwjamaica.com

Crystal Waters Villas consists of one, two or three bedroom villas each with a kitchen, dining room and patio. These villas are top-of-the-line in villa accommodations in Negril. Each room comes with a maid/cook who will tend to your every need but you have to pay for the food. If you want a high-end rental where you will have top-of-the-line accommodations, you will not go wrong choosing this hotel.

Donaldson's Inn on the Beach 4 out of 5

http://www.donaldsonsinn.com/

Phone: 876-957-4377

Email: revauds@aol.com

Donaldson's Inn on the Beach is run by the Donaldson family and is a very nice family run resort. The rooms are clean and safe and you will be comfortable staying here. This is the place to stay if you want to get away from it all.

Doris' Rooms No ratings

Web Site: none

Phone: 876-957-4215

876-281-0787

Email: none

Doris Rooms is one of the smallest hotels on Seven Mile Beach. Doris passed away several years ago but her son runs the place now. If you feel adventurous, show up with some cash and negotiate a price. I bet you could get a room for about $20 a night.

Errol's Sunset Café and Guesthouse Hostel 3 out of 5

15 Rooms

http://www.aplusjimages.com/errols/

Phone: 876-838-2448

Email: contact@errolssunset.com

When you stay at Errol's your cottage will be about 20 steps to the beach. The guesthouses are rustic and what old Negril used to be like. If you are adventurous and want to experience old-school Jamaica, Errol's would not be a bad choice.

Firefly Beach Cottages 3 out of 5

2 Rooms, 18 Suites

http://jamaicalink.com/

Phone: 876-957-4358

876-957-9325

Email: firefly@jamaicalink.com

Firefly Beach Cottages offer a clothing optional stay where you can stay and swim in the ocean or Jacuzzi au natural. If you are offended by nudity, this is not your place. The rooms are clean and it is relatively inexpensive to stay at these cottages.

Foote Prints Hotel 3 out of 5

26 Rooms, 4 Suites

http://www.footeprints.net/

Phone: 888-790-5264 (Toll Free US)

      0-800-7297-2900 (Toll Free UK)

      876-957-4300

      876-957-3132

Email: reservations@footeprints.net

Foote Prints has four different types of rooms with the top two rooms each having a kitchenette. As with most places in Negril some people love this place but some people hate it as well. If you are looking for a clean and inexpensive place to stay on the beach, this would not be a bad choice.

Freedom Villa 4 out of 5

5 Rooms

http://www.freedomvilla-negril.com/eng_impressum.htm

Phone: 876-957-3054

Email: john_maica@cwjamaica.com

Freedom Villa has a kitchen and living room that all guests share. It is located across the street from Seven Mile Beach. If you want a clean, comfortable and nice place to stay, albeit not on the beach, then this is the place to rent. You will have beach access from the properties across the street from Freedom Villa. The only reason this place does not get five stars is because of the lack of amenities.

Fun Holiday Beach Resort All-Inclusive 3 out of 5

45 Rooms

http://funholidaybeachresort.com/

Phone: 876-957-9688

876-957-3585

Email: funholidaybeachresort@cwjamaica.com

Fun Holiday Beach resort offers both an all-inclusive plan as well as a European plan, which means you pay for only the room and all food and drinks are extra. This hotel is not run by a large corporation and it does not have the same nice amenities that the larger all-inclusive hotels have. If you choose the all-inclusive package it is not like other places, there seems to be set meals and only certain drinks you can order. If you want something inexpensive but still have your meals paid for, then this would be a good choice. If you want a dazzling all-inclusive experience there are other options available.

Gardenia Resort 3 out of 5

75 Rooms

http://www.gardeniaresortnegril.com/

Phone: 876-957-4394

Email: gardeniaresort@hotmail.com

The Gardenia Resort is located across the street from Seven Mile Beach. Each room comes with free breakfast in the morning. There are rooms available with kitchenettes so you can cook your own meals. The place is run by a couple of French Canadians but the place feels like old Negril. If you want clean, safe but rustic rooms and do not care if you are directly on the beach, then this hotel will work for you.

Gatehouse Villa 4.5 out of 5

4 Rooms

http://www.gatehousevilla.com/

Phone: 435-658-1094

Email: info@gatehousevilla.com

The Gatehouse Villa is one large building with four large bedrooms, each with its own bathroom and shower. There is a nice shared kitchen and living room area. The villa is located in the middle of Seven Mile Beach. Tony's bar is located on the beach in front if these villas and is a rustic little bar where Tony will sometimes cook you a meal (jerk chicken). Gatehouse Villa is a great and inexpensive place to stay for an upscale experience.

The Golden Sunset Villas 3 out of 5

21 Rooms

http://thegoldensunset.com/

Phone: 876-957-4241

Email: arthursr@cwjamaica.com

The Golden Sunset is a moderately priced villa located across the street from Seven Mile Beach. People that go there love it, although most everyone comments on the fact that the villas need some refreshing. If you want to rent an inexpensive but clean villa, cheaper than most other villas, then this is the place for you.

Grand Lido Resort All-Inclusive Adult Only 4 out of 5

210 Rooms, all suites

http://grandlidoresorts.com/

Phone: 855-744-8374 (Toll Free US)

       876-957-5010

Email: Form on website

Grand Lido Resort used to be called Breezes and it is an all-inclusive adults-only resort that is upscale with free water sport activities that has everything a traveler could need in one location. There are multiple dining options, multiple bars and a few swimming pools to boot. It is located on Bloody Bay which is just North of Seven Mile Beach. There is a clothing optional side to this hotel as well.

Since this hotel changed owners they have worked hard to improve the hotel and the grounds. It used to be more run-down but it is coming along nicely.

Grand Pineapple Resort All-Inclusive 4 out of 5

http://www.grandpineapple.com/resorts/grand-pineapple-negril/resort-home/

Phone: 877-846-3290

      305-284-1300 (Outside North America)

Email: Form on website

The Grand Pineapple is located on Seven Mile Beach and is an inexpensive option for those who want a nice, clean all-inclusive resort. There is a beautiful seaside restaurant with a bar on site as well. This hotel was renovated and re-opened in December, 2012. If you want a nice all-inclusive hotel at a great price, this is the place to go while in Jamaica.

Greenleaf Cabins and Devon House 2.5 out of 5

11 Cabins and 2 Houses

http://www.greenleafcabins.com/

Phone: 860-621-2417 (U.S. number)

    876-957-4677

    876-957-4666

Email: maryann@greenleafcabins.com

    jjjames@greenlcafcabins.com

Greenleaf Cabins is located across the street from Seven Mile Beach and they have multiple options for family and friends who want to stay there. Some cabins with shared bathrooms go for as little as $20 a night. For $35 a night you can get a room with a bathroom. If you have a lot of people traveling with you, then rent a house which both run $180 a night and have three bedrooms and a housekeeper, cable and air conditioning.

Hedonism II All-Inclusive Adults Only 4 out of 5

280 Rooms

http://www.hedonism.com/

Phone: 631-LUV-HEDO (US)

    631-588-4336 (US)

Canadian Email: sales.canada@superclubs.com

UK and Europe Email: info@hedonism.com

Hedonism has both a nude and prude side, which is pretty self-explanatory. This is not the resort for you if you do not like nudity or are iffy about any other adult themed activities. Recent posts from travelers there say that the resort is getting a little ragged around the edges and that the resort needs an update. The food is outstanding and water activities are included in the price you pay. Children are obviously not allowed at this property.

Hidden Paradise 4 out of 5

22 Rooms

http://www.hidden-paradise.com/

Phone: 876-957-3370

876-957-4404

Email: Jamaica@hidden-paradise.com

Hidden Paradise is located across the street from Seven Mile Beach but it has a restaurant called Mama Flo's that is located on the beach, and you have complete beach access in front of Mama Flo's. If you are looking for an inexpensive and safe place to stay, this would be it. Remember, you are not on the beach but this means the rates are cheaper.

Idle Awhile 4.5 out of 5

16 Rooms

http://www.idleawhile.com/index.htm

Phone: 877-243-5352 (Toll Free US)

876-957-3302

Email: stay@idleawhile.com

Idle Awhile is very much a boutique hotel located on Seven Mile Beach. If you are looking for a fantastic little hotel that is not all-inclusive, then this hotel should be at the top of your list. The rooms are nice sized and in great shape and the reviews are glowing.

Jah B's Doll House Cottages 3 out of 5

http://www.realnegril.com/jahbs/

Phone: 876-957-4235

Email: joycesresturant@yahoo.com

Jah B's Doll House Cottages is located across the street from Seven Mile Beach. It is a rustic place with rustic cottages that can be had for very low prices. If you stay here be forewarned that this is a rustic old Negril-type accommodation. If you are adventurous and are looking for the old Negril, this place fits the bill.

Jamaica Tamboo Resort 4.5 out of 5

16 Rooms

http://www.jamaicatambooresort.com/

Phone: 876-957-4282

Email: jamaica_tamboo@yahoo.com

Jamaica Tamboo Resort is a small hotel with 16 rooms. It is located on Seven Mile Beach and the rooms are clean and comfortable.

Kuyaba on the Beach 4 out of 5

22 Rooms

http://www.kuyaba.com/

Phone: 876-957-4318

876-957-9815

Email: kuyaba@cwjamaica.com

Kuyaba on the Beach is a clean, basic and rustic place to stay if you want to stay on Seven Mile Beach. The cottages are cute and the grounds are stunning and very tropical. The only downside is that the property is surrounded on both sides by music clubs so bring your ear plugs.

Lazy Dayz 3.5 out of 5

12 Rooms

http://www.lazydayznegril.com/

Phone: 905-826-2079

Email: Negril@passport.ca

Lazy Dayz was the place I stayed when I first went to Negril so it holds a special place in my heart. The rooms are like cabins and some are built high and up in the trees. The rooms are basic and clean and some rooms have a shared bathroom. Lazy Dayz is located next to Niah's Patties which may be enough to convince you to stay here.

Legends Beach Resort All-Inclusive 3.5 out of 5

25 Rooms

http://www.negrilhotels.com/default.htm

Phone: 315-636-4390 (US)

       876-957-4395

Email: stay@negrilhotels.com

Legends Beach Resort is an all-inclusive but most of the reviews I have read recommended staying away from that option. There is no traditional buffet, just a few options for dinner that are not very appealing. They do have a sister resort called Samsara at the Cliffs of Negril where there are exchange privileges, so if you are bored or looking for a change of pace then this is an option.

Lily Mae's Guest House No ratings

Web Site: none

Phone: 876-957-4762

Email: none

Lily Mae's Guesthouse is the hardest place to get information about that I have ever run across. I got the phone number and email address from a German web site and that is the only information available. It is located across the street from Seven Mile Beach and as far as I can tell there have been no reviews about this place. It must mean it is truly rustic and old Negril!

Update: I called Lily Mae's Guest House in June of 2014 and they are open and the phone number listed above is valid. They have no web presence at all so the only way to get a room is to call.

Mariposa Hideaway 2 out of 5

20 Rooms

http://www.mariposahideaway.com/

Phone: 876-957-4918

Email: mariposa@cwjamaica.com

Mariposa Hideaway is located on Seven Mile Beach. It offers free breakfast with every reservation. The current reviews describe a place that needs a little work but would be fine for those looking for a basic room.

Merril's I, Merril's II and Merril's III All-Inclusive 3 out of 5

189 Rooms total

http://www.merrilsbeachresorts.com/

http://www.merrilsbeach.com

Phone: 305-945-4774

Email: info@merrilsbeachresorts.com

Merril's Resorts are three different resorts, two that are next to each other and the third that is separated by one other resort. This is an all-inclusive resort where if you stay at one you will have privileges at all three. This is not a top-of-the-line all-inclusive, but it isn't bad, especially if you are on a budget.

Mom's Place 4 out of 5

7 Rooms

http://www.momsnegriljamaica.com/

Phone: 876-957-3349

Email: momsplace32@hotmail.com

Mom's Place is located on Seven Mile Beach and is a small family run resort. It is like a small motel you would find in the states. It is more than a cottage or a cabin, but smaller than even a medium sized hotel. They do not take credit cards so bring plenty of cash. This is a nice family run place to stay on the beach.

Moonrise Villas 3.5 out of 5

17 Rooms

www.moornrisevillas.com

Phone: 876-957-4344

876-897-1953 (Cell)

876-284-3473 (Cell)

Email: moonrisevillas@yahoo.com

Moonrise Villas is located across the street from Seven Mile Beach. The price for a room there is about $60 a night. Some of the villas have kitchenettes in them so you do not have to eat out for every meal. The landscaping is lush and tropical and the rooms are clean and presentable.

Negril Beach Club (Mariner's Negril Beach Club) 3 out of 5

49 Rooms

http://www.negrilbeachcondo.com/

Phone: 954-840-7119 (US)

    876-957-4323

    876-578-7992

Email: negrilcondo@hotmail.com

I have stayed at the Negril Beach Club twice and both times I have had good experiences. The hotel is part of a condominium complex so most rooms have a kitchenette. Some rooms are for rent but most were sold as time shares. The rooms can be dated but they are clean and the beach is about the biggest and best you will find in Negril. Since some of the units are condos that are owned, there is no exact figure for the number of rooms available for rent.

Negril Palms Resort 3.5 out of 5

34 Rooms

http://www.palmsjamaica.com/

Phone: 800-249-5988 (Toll Free US and Canada)

876-957-4375

Email: reservations@negrilpalmshotel.com

The Palms Resort is located on Seven Mile Beach and has recently undergone renovations. From previous reviews it sounded like it needed a freshening. If you are looking for a nice little place right on the beach then this could be the place for you.

Negril Tree House (Negril Cabins Resort) 4.5 out of 5

70 Rooms

http://www.negril-treehouse.com/

Phone: 876-957-4287

Email: info@negril-treehouse.com

When you stay at the Negril Tree House, breakfast is included in the price. The Tree House is one of the nicer properties in Negril that is not all-inclusive or not a villa. The hotel is located on Seven Mile Beach and the reviews for this place are outstanding.

Negril Villa (at White Sands Negril) No Ratings

1 Room

http://www.whitesandsjamaica.com/rooms/villa/

Phone: 305-503-9074 (US)

876-957-4291

Email: whitesands@cwjamaica.com

The Negril Villa is a 10 person retreat that is located across the street from Seven Mile Beach and is part of White Sands Negril. It has 4 bedrooms and 4 bathrooms. If you have a big group or family this would be the perfect place to stay. When you stay here you have access to everything at White Sands.

Nirvana on the Beach Cottages 4.5 out of 5

12 Rooms

http://www.nirvananegril.com/

Phone: 941-708-02503 November 1st to May 20th US Florida phone

716-789-5955 May 20th to November 1st US phone

Email: info@nirvananegril.com

Nirvana on the Beach features 5 cottages and 7 one bedroom suites directly on Seven Mile Beach. The cottages have two or three bedrooms and kitchenettes. There is no AC in the cottages, just ceiling fans. One meal per day is included in the cottage rental but you have to provide the food. Nirvana is run and owned by a couple who live in Florida. Nirvana is one of the top five resorts on

Negril's Seven Mile Beach.

Ocean Wave Villa

 4.0 out of 5

6 Rooms

http://www.oceanwavevilla.net/

Phone: 876-483-0232

Email: info@oceanwavevilla.net

This villa is listed under two different names on the web so I chose the most prevalent one. This villa is located across the street from Seven Mile Beach near the middle of Seven Mile Beach. Each villa can accommodate between two to four people, depending on the villa. Each villa has a kitchenette with all the amenities needed to cook your own meals. The villa is run and owned by a family and you will get a family feel when you book here. There is a small but seasonal restaurant and a small bar, but there are plenty of options across the street and on the beach. There is a small laundry that you can use but you have to supply your own soap. This villa is a very nice place to stay.

Our Past Time Villas 4 out of 5

17 Rooms

http://www.ourpasttimenegril.com/

Phone: 876-957-5422

636-448-8185 (US Reservations)

Email: info@ourpasttimenegril.com

Our Past Time is located right on Seven Mile Beach up towards the Northern end near Hedonism II. It is a nice and quiet place to relax and play and the prices are very, very nice for this level of hotel. If you are looking for something akin to a nice, but not super fancy, hotel in the States, then this would be the ideal place.

Perseverance No Ratings

24 Rooms (if you include BT's Resort)

http://www.go-jam.com/perseverance-e.html

Phone: 876-957-4333

876-957-4744 from 9:00 AM to 9:00 PM

Email: info@go-jam.com

Perseverance is located across the street from Seven Mile Beach and is run with a resort called BT's Resort. It is truly a rustic place to stay and room rates as of this writing are $20 a night or $120 per week U.S. Bathrooms are either shared, outside or private. The more you pay the more privacy you get with the bathrooms. If you simply want a no-frills room cheap, this is the place for you.

Pure Garden Resort (formerly Bungalo Hotel) 2 out of 5

40 Rooms

http://www.purenegril.com/

Phone: 876-957-4767

Email: info@purenegril.com

The Pure garden Resort is located across the street from Seven Mile Beach. There are two types of rooms, one with two double beds and the other type of room has a kitchenette. If you are looking for a cheap place to stay and do not mind being across the street from the beach, then this is the place for you.

Rayon Hotel 4.5 out of 5

21 Rooms

http://www.rayonhotel.com/

Phone: 876-957-9166

Email: sales@rayonhotels.com

The Rayon Hotel is located across the street from Seven Mile Beach. If you are looking for something other than rustic accommodations across the street from Seven Mile Beach, then this is your place. It is a nice little hotel that is cheaper to stay at than comparable hotels that are on the beach. Breakfast is included in your room cost. This is a very nice place, but not on the beach.

RIU Palace Tropical Bay All-Inclusive 5 out of 5

396 Rooms

http://www.riu.com/en/Paises/jamaica/negril/hotel-riu-tropical-bay/index.jsp

Phone: 888-RIU-4990 (Toll Free US)

876-957-5900

Email: hotel.tropicalbay@riu.com

The RIU hotels are both located on Bloody Bay which is connected to Seven Mile Beach at the North end of the beach. RIU hotels are all-inclusive and both have several different restaurants, bars and pool areas. When you stay at one you have privileges at the other's bars and restaurants.

Rondel Village 4.5 out of 5

40 Rooms

http://rondelvillage.com/

Phone: 876-957-4413

Email: info@rondelvillage.com

Rondel Village is a beautiful little boutique hotel located right on Seven Mile Beach. The hotel is architecturally beautiful and the grounds are lush and well-maintained. This is one of the nicer properties in Negril. This hotel has a lot of returning customers each year which is a very good indication of the quality of the stay there.

Rooms on the Beach 4 out of 5

57 Rooms

http://www.roomsresorts.com/negril.asp

Phone: 877-467-8737 (Toll Free US)

Email: none

Rooms on the Beach is located right on Seven Mile Beach in Negril. They do not have wireless internet so if you need internet access you have to use their internet café. This hotel is run by the same company that runs Breezes Resorts and Hedonism. They do have a laundry room at this resort which can be used for a small fee. This is a great quality hotel that can be booked for an inexpensive price. If you want quality at a great price then this should be the place you stay. Your stay here includes free breakfast.

Roots Bamboo 3.5 out of 5

14 Rooms and campsite

http://www.rootsbamboobeach.com

Phone: 876-957-4479

      876-417-1595 (Cell)

Email: reservations@rootsbamboo.com

      Denise.plummer64@hotmail.com

Roots Bamboo is a rustic and charming little place located on Seven Mile Beach. Rooms are small and quaint and start at $35 a night. You can camp there if you are single for $12 a night, or $23 a night for a double. You need to supply the tent. If you want truly rustic and old Negril Charm then this is the place for you. Small, rustic and on the beach will transport you back to old Negril.

Sandals Negril Beach Resort All-Inclusive 5 out of 5

223 Rooms

http://www.sandals.com/main/negril/ne-home.cfm

Phone: 888-726-3257 (Toll Free US)

Email: Form on website

Sandals is located on Seven Mile Beach just South of Bloody Bay. Sandals Resorts are some of the finest all-inclusive resorts you can find anywhere. Activities that are included in the price are SCUBA diving and snorkeling, along with water skiing, wind surfing, and going out on a glass bottomed boat. Everything is included in your price, including round trip transportation to the airport. You can spend up to $600 dollars a night on their most expensive room. If you want to stay at the best place, this would be it. Every one of your needs will be taken care of at Sandals.

Sandy Haven 4.5 out of 5

35 Rooms

http://www.sandyhavenresort.com/

Phone: 876-957-3200

800-583-8365 (toll free U.S)

Email: Form on website

Sandy Haven is a luxury boutique hotel located on Seven Mile Beach. If you want to go to one of the top hotels in Negril, but you also want to stay at someplace smaller than Sandals, then this would be a great choice. It is family run and simply beautiful.

Sea Sand Eco Villas 4.5 out of 5

4 Rooms

http://www.seasandecovillas.com

Phone: 876-957-9789

Email: seasandecovillas@gmail.com

Sea Sand Eco Villas is located right on Seven Mile Beach. With each villa rental there comes a maid who will cook and clean for you, as well as do your laundry. You have to buy the groceries. The Villas have one, two, three, or four bedrooms. The price is very reasonable, and works out to a little over $100 a couple if you find friends to go and stay with you. The price includes the maid who will cook for you. I cannot say enough good things about staying at this resort.

Sea Splash Resort 4 out of 5

15 Rooms

http://www.seasplash.com/

Phone: 888-790-5264 (Toll Free US)

00-800-7297-2900 (Toll Free UK)

876-957-4041

Email: seasplash@cwjamaica.com

Sea Splash Resort is located on Seven Mile Beach in Negril. This property was recently renovated and is an excellent choice to stay for a mid-priced hotel. Breakfast is complimentary. The rooms are nice sized and recently refurbished. This is a nice choice for a reasonable price.

Sea Wind Resort All-Inclusive option 5 out of 5

29 Rooms

http://www.seawindresortjamaica.com/

Phone: 876-957-9018

Email: Form on website

Sea Wind Resort is one of the top five places to stay on Seven Mile Beach. This hotel has an all-inclusive option if that is what you prefer. The rooms are very nice, well-kept, clean and affordable. While not the same as a larger all-inclusive, the food is good but is not served buffet-style. This hotel is consistently rated in the top five according to guests who stay there.

Secrets Cabins 4.5 out of 5

4 Cabins

http://www.jamaicalink.com/secrets/

Phone: 876-957-4358

876-957-9325

Email: secrets@jamaicalink.com

Secrets is located in the middle of the Firefly property and consists of four very nice cabins on Seven Mile Beach. This place is rustic and you will share a bathroom with other guests. Nudity is permitted at Firefly and here. The best part of the rustic experience at Secrets is that it only costs about $30 a night to stay here and you are right near the beach. If you want cheap, rustic, beautiful, and safe, then this is a great place to stay.

Shields Negril Villas 3 out of 5

36 Rooms

http://shieldsnegril.net/

Phone: 888-790-5264 (Toll Free US)

0-800-7297-2900 (Toll free UK)

876-957-3112

876-783-9038

Email: reservations@shieldsnegril.net

Shields Negril Villas is located on Seven Mile Beach close to the town of Negril. You have a choice of a standard room, a one bedroom with a kitchenette or a two bedroom with a kitchenette. Shields is a clean and comfortable place to stay that is relatively inexpensive.

Sunquest Cottages (Formerly Wild Parrot Beach Cottages) 4.5 out of 5

14 Rooms

Web Site: none

Phone: 876-957-4470

Email: none

Sunquest Cottages (Formerly Wild Parrot Beach Cottages) is located almost in the middle on Seven Mile Beach. It is one of the nicer cottages that you will find on the beach. The rooms are clean and comfortable. It is a homey little place that will make you feel at home when you stay here.

Sunrise Club 4 out of 5

14 Rooms

http://www.sunriseclub.com/

Phone: 876-957-4293

Email: info@sunriseclub.com

The Sunrise Club is located across the street from Seven Mile Beach. The rooms are clean and comfortable and cheap. The Sunrise Club is a step above the rustic cottages that dot Seven Mile Beach, but it is also across the street from the beach. People that stay here love it.

Sunset at the Palms All-Inclusive 5 out of 5

86 Rooms

http://www.sunsetatthepalms.com/

Phone: 877-734-3486 (Toll Free US)

     876-979-8800

Email: Form on website

Sunset at the Palms is located across the street from Seven Mile Beach. All rooms are built like tree houses so it is a unique all-inclusive experience. I have seen this place described as an all-inclusive boutique hotel. If you stay here bring bug spray because the grounds are lush and tropical and there are some mosquitos. Sunset at the Palms is truly unique, from the rooms and vibe of the place, to being an all-inclusive package that does not feel too big. It is across the street from the beach but there is usually a crossing guard near the property to stop traffic. This is a great choice if you do not want a humungous all-inclusive experience.

Sunset on the Beach Hotel (also known as Coral Seas Beach) 4 out of 5

32 Rooms

http://www.coralseasresort.com

Phone: 888-790-5264 (Toll Free US)

0-800-7297-2900 (Toll Free UK)

876-957-9226

Email: reservations@coralseasresort.com

The Coral Seas consists of two different hotels, the Coral Seas Beach (also known as Sunset Beach) and the Coral Seas Garden. The Coral Seas Beach is located on Seven Mile Beach, near the town of Negril, while the Coral Seas Garden is located across the street from the beach further to the north. When you reserve rooms here the transportation from the airport is included and is in a very nice limousine.

Top Beach Cabins Rooms and Bar 5 out of 5

http://www.oocities.org/topbeachcabins/main.html

Phone: 876-957-3138

876-834-4466 (Cell)

Email: topbeachcabins@hotmail.com

Top beach Cabins are very unique in that all the rooms have an ocean view and their own private balcony. All the rooms also have a kitchenette in them. This place is right on Seven Mile Beach and the rooms are more upscale than the word "cabins" in the name would suggest. The kitchenettes are very nice compared to most places in Negril. On top of all this, the rates are very reasonable. This would be a very nice choice for anyone, and especially if you are looking to stay in a smaller family run hotel.

Travelers Hotel Beach Resort **4 out of 5**

42 Rooms

http://www.travellersresorts.com/

Phone: 718-514-6031 (US Number)

      876-957-3039

Email: reservations@tbresorts.com

Travelers Hotel Beach Resort is located on Seven Mile Beach close to the town of Negril. They have a normal hotel like you would find anywhere else in the U.S., but they also have more rustic cabins on site as well. We had friends stay at this hotel and they were in one of the rustic cabins. The main problem they had with their cabin was the noise that came from the bar area until 2:00 AM and the fitness center noise at 6:00 AM. If you stay in the cabins bring ear plugs.

Tropical Fantasy: **No Ratings**

No website

Phone: 876-957-4764

      876-899-7855 (cell)

Email: tropicalfantasy_55@hotmail.com (she only answers her emails once a week)

Tropical Fantasy is located across the street from Seven Mile Beach behind the Boat Bar. All of their cabins have in suite bathrooms and you can rent some of them by the month. This is a rustic little place, across the street from the beach, and people who have stayed there like it. It is very rustic.

Valentine Villas @ Trombone's Place 5 out of 5

7 Rooms

http://www.valentinevillas.com/

Phone: 631-704-9356 (US number)

      876-562-8435

Email: valentinevillas@aol.com

Valentine Villas is located on Seven Mile Beach and consists of one main villa with three rooms, one facing the ocean with a full kitchen, and two garden view rooms with no kitchen. There are also four rooms for rent in back that they call Trombone's Boardhouse that are rustic, but each one has their own private bathroom. This place is clean and comfortable and very well-liked by people who have been there. If you are looking for a laid back place to stay, this would be a great choice.

Villa Mora 4 out of 5

2 Rooms

http://www.villamoranegril.net/

Phone: 866-626-6816 (Toll Free US)

Email: info@villamoranegril.net

The Villa Mora is a three bedroom cottage with daily maid service. It is located across the street from Seven Mile Beach. The place rents by the week and is basically a house that you will have to yourself.

Whistling Bird 4 out of 5

12 Rooms

http://www.whistlingbird.info

Phone: 800-460-4042 (Toll Free US)

      876-957-4403

Email: whistlingbird@negriljamaica.com

Whistling Bird is located on Seven Mile Beach and offers many different options on room. There are cottages with one room all the way up to a main guest house that has six rooms. You can also pay for breakfast, breakfast and dinner, and an all-inclusive option. Whistling Bird is one of the first resorts to exist in Negril and it has a lot of charm.

White Sands 4 out of 5

40 Rooms

http://www.whitesandsjamaica.com/

Phone: 305-503-9074 (a Miami number that rings directly in Jamaica)

    876-957-4291

Email: whitesands@cwjamaica.com

White Sands Negril is located on Seven Mile Beach. There are room options there where you can get your own kitchenette. The place is well-run and people who have stayed there keep coming back. This is a very nice mid-sized hotel that is on the beach.

Yellow Bird 3.5 out of 5

15 Rooms

http://www.theyellowbird.com/

Phone: 876-957-4252

    876-381-3648

Email: Form on web site

The Yellow Bird is most often described as "quaint." It is located on Seven Mile Beach and consists of guest rooms and cottages. The buildings are close to the beach. If you want a nice clean room in a safe environment, yet also want to experience a little bit of rustic Negril, then this is the place for you.

Yoga Center 5 out of 5

12 Rooms

http://www.negrilyoga.com/

Phone: 239-566-2284 (US)

      876-957-4397

Email: Form on website

The Yoga Center is located across the street from Seven Mile Beach and it is one of the closest hotels to the town of Negril. This is the place to stay if you want a spa/yoga center experience. The restaurant provides natural and fresh food so you can tend to your physical side as well as your spiritual side. Yoga classes cost $15 if you do not stay here or $10 per session if you are a guest.

Negril Jamaica Checklist

Here is a list of the most common things you will need when you travel to Jamaica. The list is fairly comprehensive for most travelers but it your needs may be slightly different than what is on this list.

Passport: If your passport is going to expire within 6 months of your trip, you must apply for a new passport. You will not be able to enter Jamaica if your passport is set to expire within six months.

Visa: If you come from the US you do not need a travel visa. If you come from countries other than the US you may need a travel visa. Check with your government to see if this is the case.

Money

Credit Cards

Prescription Medications

Sunscreen: Bring enough to get you through the entire stay because it is expensive in Negril. Bring sunscreen with high SPF values so you do not burn. If you go in the pools or ocean be sure to bring sunscreen that is waterproof. Even if you do not use the water it might be a good idea to bring waterproof sunscreen because you will sweat a lot.

Swimsuits

Shorts

Shirts

Dress pants

Jeans

Light Jacket or Sweatshirt

Sunglasses

Collapsible Cooler

Re-freezable ice packs for your cooler

Blender with a cooler on top if you want to make beach drinks

Computer (for internet access)

Camera

Batteries for camera if no charger

Books to read or your Kindle or other e-book reader, if you are a reader

Exercise clothes if you are going to do yoga or running

Underwear and socks

IBSN: 978-1-46817-978-1

Contact the Author

If you have any questions or suggestions for this book I would love to hear your comments. Please email me at scotthanse@gmail.com and put "Negril Vacations in the subject line.

Visit our fan page at:

http://www.facebook.com/pages/Negril-Beach-Vacations/222668484476044

Made in the USA
San Bernardino, CA
08 January 2016